THE
RELEVANCE
OF
RELIGION

THE
RELEVANCE
OF
RELIGION

HOW FAITHFUL PEOPLE
CAN CHANGE POLITICS

JOHN DANFORTH

RANDOM HOUSE

NEW YORK

Published in the United States by Random House, an imprint
and division of Penguin Random House LLC, New York.

RANDOM HOUSE and the HOUSE colophon are registered
trademarks of Penguin Random House LLC.

Library of Congress Cataloging-in-Publication Data
Danforth, John C.
The relevance of religion : how faithful people can change politics /
John Danforth.
pages   cm
ISBN 978-0-8129-9790-3
eBook ISBN 978-0-8129-9791-0
1. Christianity and politics—United States.   2. Christians—Political activity—
United States.   I. Title.
BR516.D25 2015
261.70973—dc23
2015013178

Printed in the United States of America on acid-free paper

randomhousebooks.com

2 4 6 8 9 7 5 3 1

First Edition

Title-page images: copyright © iStock.com/© michaelquirk (left),
© serazetdinov (right)

Book design by Victoria Wong

To Alex Netchvolodoff

CONTENTS

PROLOGUE

Fixing Broken Government

Religion in politics can be a negative or a positive. A decade ago, I wrote *Faith and Politics,* a book that emphasized the negative and argued that the exploitation of wedge issues for the purpose of energizing the base of the Republican Party was dividing and harming the country. This book, by contrast, emphasizes the positive and attempts to show how religion can play an important and constructive part in American politics. It is written for people of faith who are concerned that our government is dysfunctional, who believe that their religion offers much of importance for them to say, and who think that they have a duty to help make government work.

The well-deserved attention the negative has received, not only from me but from Madeleine Albright, E. J. Dionne, and others, has had the salutary effect of decreasing the misuse of religion for political purposes. Playing to religious passions is easier done discreetly than in the glare of public attention it has recently received. The alarm that some have expressed at what they see as the decline of religion in America is, in part, a recognition that the energy of last decade's religiously fraught issues such as embryonic stem cell research and end-of-life care has lost much of its steam. Even the hot-button subject of gay marriage isn't as hot as it was just a few years ago, with an increasing percentage of our population now accepting of or at least resigned to the new reality. Big issues eventually become old ones as public passion grows and then dissipates. What I and others wrote about divisive religious issues contributed to this maturing process, and it was in line with an American tradition dating from Jefferson and Madison that warned against the entanglement of religion and politics.

My one-sided emphasis on the negative, on the dangerous divisiveness of religion in the public square, was unsatisfying to some people who take religion seriously and believe that it should influence all of life, including politics. Their belief is squarely within the biblical tradition that calls faithful people to engage themselves actively in the world.

The Old Testament tells of a leader who confronted Pharaoh, a people who went to war, and prophets who spoke truth to kings. This activist understanding of religion carried into the New Testament. Jesus repeatedly told his disciples that faith was more than a private matter. They were expected to do things, to invest their talents, to bear fruit, to turn seeds into high-yielding grain. They were to go into the world and make disciples. Nowhere does the Bible suggest that the responsibility of religion is to stay out of people's hair.

But that is exactly how some people understandably took what I said a decade ago. After I had expressed concern that the Christian right had taken over the Republican Party, Rush Limbaugh claimed that I want religious people to get out of politics. In fact, that is the opposite of what I want. I want political people to stop using religion to divide Americans, but I want religious people to become more engaged in fixing politics that is currently broken. And as the American people clearly understand, today's politics is most certainly broken.

Nearly every day, I hear variations of the same comment: "I bet you don't miss it"—"it" meaning Washington, D.C., which I left when I retired from the Senate in 1994. What's interesting is both the certainty and the frequency with which people make that comment today. Even when put as a question—"Do you miss it?"—there is a rhetorical ring, as if to say, "Of course you don't miss Washington, how could you?" As for frequency, I don't recall hearing people say this in my early post-Washington years. Back then, some people wondered if the slow pace of Congress could be frustrating, but there wasn't what now appears to be a universal assumption that service in Congress is such a miserable condition that any sane person would head for the exit.

After I announced that I would be retiring from the Senate, I made a final tour of Missouri to thank my constituents for electing me. I told them that I loved my years in office, and that I was retiring only because I thought it was time to come home. That was true. I did love it then, and I would hate it now. When people bet I don't miss the Senate, they are expressing a widespread belief that government is ill serving the nation. In October 2013, Pew Research Center reported that only 19 percent of Americans say that they trust government to do what is right at least most of the time. Simultaneously, Pew reported that 81 percent of the public was dissatisfied with the state of the nation.*

Some religious people, Mennonites for example, separate themselves entirely from the world of politics. But many—I believe most—religious people believe that their faith relates to all of life: to their community, to their world, and to their politics. Today the faithful, de-

---

* Pew Research Center, "Trust in Government Nears Record Low, but Most Federal Agencies Are Viewed Favorably," October 18, 2013, www.people-press.org/2013/10/18/trust-in-government-nears-record-low-but-most-federal-agencies-are-viewed-favorably/; Pew Research Center, "As Debt Deadline Nears, Concern Ticks Up but Skepticism Persists," October 15, 2013, www.people-press.org/2013/10/15/as-debt-limit-deadline-nears-concern-ticks-up-but-skepticism-persists/.

spite some sharp differences on important questions of moral principle, share a common sense that something is terribly wrong in American politics, and they want to make it right.

They sense that government has become nothing more than a grab bag for interest groups wherein politicians will do whatever it takes to keep themselves in office.

They sense that Americans are losing what has connected us, that individualistic isolation is suffocating community, that we are holing up in front of our television sets, that as modern communication and transportation make the world smaller, we are dispersing to the suburbs and growing further apart.

They sense that government doesn't work, that every issue devolves into endless bickering, that the permanent condition of politics is gridlock.

"Gridlock" is an expressive term, because, like cars stuck in traffic, government seems incapable of moving in any direction. The national debt approaches $20 trillion, and there is no real effort to contain it. In most years, Congress doesn't pass a budget controlling how much government should tax and spend, and it doesn't pass appropriations bills to decide where to do the spending. For decades we have known that our most important domestic programs, Social Security and Medicare, are unsustainable on their present course, yet nothing is

done to change course. Twelve million or so illegal immigrants reside in our country, and more arrive daily, but
government cannot enact an immigration policy. Our
roads and bridges deteriorate without Washington's response. In foreign affairs, Russia reverts to its czarist am-
bitions and Islamist radicals proclaim a caliphate, while
our belief that political divisions should end at the water's edge is a distant memory.

It's not that nobody in politics has an idea of what to
do about these challenges. Everyone seems to have a different one, and all of them are mutually exclusive. Members of Congress appear on Sunday talk shows and
present their ideas with great passion, while we watch
them and say to ourselves, "This is just political. It isn't
going anywhere."

The liberal among us often have confidence that by
enacting the right policies, government has solutions to
America's problems. Conservatives tend to be more skep-
tical about the efficacy of big programs. But all of us, no
matter our ideology, want government that works and is
capable of moving in some direction, however imper-
fectly. It seems to all of us that a government that works is
the least we should be able to expect from our politicians.

It would be easy to go on at length lamenting the state
of politics, but that would only plant the idea that all is
hopeless and we might as well give up. Such cynicism

would be a terrible disservice to the country. Whatever our sense that something is wrong, an overwhelming majority of our people say they are proud to be Americans. So when politics is broken, we should mend it. That is the mission of religious people who are engaged in politics—fix it, make things better.

As we shall see in the discussion of our first four presidents, Americans have long believed that in even the best of times under the best-designed system of government something essential would be missing that could never be supplied by government alone. This is so because the essence of politics is attending to and balancing self-interests, and, as our founders acknowledged, containing interests would not suffice to sustain the nation. What is missing in politics alone is the commitment to look beyond the self and serve the common good, and behind such commitment is the healing power of religion.

Sailing to the New World in 1630, John Winthrop—a layman, not a clergyman—preached his famous sermon with its profoundly religious message. He envisioned America as a model society where we would try to live not in service to self but for the welfare of each other. He said that the eyes of Europe would be on us, so it would be our responsibility to set an example and to conduct ourselves as "a city upon a hill." That remains our responsibility today. So if we think that America's light is today not as bright as it should be, it is our responsibility to turn up that light. For those of us who, like John Winthrop, believe that we have a purpose given to us by God, our responsibility is especially urgent.

THE
RELEVANCE
OF
RELIGION

CHAPTER ONE

A PERSONAL QUEST

In the spring of 1959, I walked into the office of Professor Browne Barr having heard from other students that he was the most pastoral teacher at Yale Divinity School. I was intent on baring my soul. I had entered the divinity school believing that God intended me for the parish clergy or for teaching religion, but I was now in a vocational crisis, dreading either career path and knowing that I lacked both the temperament of a pastor and the abstract mind of a theologian. My future seemed unbearable, and being surrounded by dedicated and contented classmates deepened my gloom.

Before my senior year in college, my aim was politics, as it had been since age ten when, sitting in the gallery of the U.S. Senate I told myself, "I want to do that someday." As a schoolboy, I signed up for every activity that was at all political: debates in the school assembly, mock nominating conventions, the model UN. I loved it. Everyone knew of my passion for politics, my parents who encouraged me and my classmates who nicknamed me "Senator." Then came college, where I majored in religion and became convinced that God wanted me to have a future in the ministry.

I entered Professor Barr's office in a quandary. God must have wanted me for the ministry or I would not have been at Yale. But did I have to do something I dreaded? Could I change course and resume the political path I loved, or was I compelled to stick it out at divinity school because to do otherwise would be disobedient to God?

Professor Barr barely looked up from his desk, never invited me to sit down, and interrupted me two or three minutes into my speech, saying, "God doesn't expect you to walk around on your knees if you don't want to." And that was it. End of meeting. He never explained what he meant. Was he telling me that God never wants us to do what we don't enjoy? That seemed unimaginable, as the Gospels teach us that disciples do what no one would want to—leave home and family, pick up our crosses, even die. So why should it be okay for me to choose politics over the ministry just because politics would give me more pleasure than, say, calling on the sick? My decision to shift to law school, then to politics, was selfish, based on my personal likes and dislikes. Maybe I should feel guilty about that, but I must admit that I have never for a minute regretted the decision. I would have been a terrible pastor.

That said, I didn't think then, and don't think now, that I should brush off my supposed call to the ministry as though it never happened. I did major in religion in college and ended up graduating from Yale with degrees in both law and divinity. Although I have never been in the full-time parish ministry, I was ordained into the priesthood of the Episcopal Church. Surely there must be some connection between my theological education and ordination on one hand and politics, which has been such a big part of my life, on the other. My life shouldn't be neatly compartmentalized between what I believe and what I do. So for nearly sixty years I have been trying to work out in my mind the relevance of my religion to my politics.

One particular question has been on my mind since as a college senior I read the work of the great twentieth-century theologian Reinhold Niebuhr. Niebuhr taught that the standard for Christian ethics is Christ's sacrificial death on the Cross. We should love one another as Christ loves us. Yet Niebuhr was realistic about human behavior. In the real world, we are seldom sacrificial. We further our own interests, and we create political systems that balance our competing interests and protect us from each other as each tries to advance his or her own causes. Politics is about balancing power, not practicing sacrificial love. Indeed, Niebuhr believed that if a political system were to practice the Love Commandment, say through pacifism, the consequence would be injustice—the dominance by the strong and fierce over the weak. Nevertheless, Niebuhr thought that while the Love Commandment could not be implemented as a plan for governing, it remained relevant as a standard for politics. Ever since I was a college senior, I have wondered how this could be so.

This book is an attempt to find out where I am in my own thinking in the hope that my struggle will help others think about the relationship between their faith and how they go about their lives as citizens and their engagement in politics.

The fact that after all these years I'm still trying to work out how my faith should affect my approach to politics shows that I have never come up with easy answers. It hasn't been as though a friend has asked, "Well, Jack, what do your religious beliefs mean for your politics?" and I could spontaneously say, "The answer is X, Y, and Z." I never thought that my religion should govern specific Senate votes on, say, tax or appropriations bills, and I don't recall any constituent suggesting that it should. Some people on the left and the right have claimed to be able to do what I could not. They have drawn causal connections between their understanding of religion and their positions on particular issues. Many conservatives have done this on social issues, saying that their religion compels opposition to abortion, embryonic stem cell research, and same-sex marriage. Many liberals have claimed that the religious mandate to care for the poor and sick leads directly to support for government welfare and health care programs. While it's important to measure all that I do, including my politics, against the demands of my faith, I have found it difficult to draw straight lines between the creeds I believe and the policies I support. On the contrary, I am convinced that the sanctification of my political opinions would amount to idolatry that would render it impossible to compromise with others.

It's possible to conceive of hypothetical circumstances where we could confidently say that a political position would be contrary to the will of God. A racist platform espoused by neo-Nazis would be an example. But in twenty-first-century America, such opinions are not within the range of serious debate, much less possible implementation. The real world of American politics consists of a series of issues on which good-hearted and reasonable people disagree, issues such as taxes, spending, and America's role in the world, issues on which vigorous disagreement is normal but moral condemnation would be out of place.

Attempts to translate religious beliefs into stands on specific issues are misguided for both religious and political reasons. From the standpoint of religion, it is both presumptuous and idolatrous to claim that one's political opinions are endorsed by God. From the standpoint of politics, such a claim closes debate and forecloses agreement.

If faithful people are to mend broken politics, the first step should be to resist the temptation to confuse religion with topical issues and turn belief into political platforms. But that's only the first step. Far more important than trying to influence any specific governmental policy is changing the tone of American politics, bridging differences rather than widening them—in short, making what is now a dysfunctional system workable. This healing ministry, not issue advocacy, can and should be the special gift of religion to America.

I'm not alone in my reluctance to identify political positions with religious beliefs. In their book *American Grace*, eminent scholars Robert Putnam and David Campbell have used public opinion surveys to show that the linkage of faith and politics by the religious right has led to a dramatic withdrawal by young adults from both formal religion and conservative politics.

So it is not my objective to persuade readers that their faith should compel them to be liberals or conservatives, Democrats or Republicans. To the contrary, my conviction that religion and politics are very different realms as well as the need to restore civility to public discourse lead me to a key point. Good and faithful people can vigorously champion opposing views on the most hotly contested issues of our time. Indeed, honoring the motives and the right of good people to disagree with one another is not just important, it is essential.

Instead of advancing a polemic for one ideology or another, my intention is to suggest a general approach religious people might take as they think about politics—broad principles, not specific policies. My hope is that we can join together in a common approach while honoring our differences on the issues of the day.

I believe there are four fundamental concepts that faithful people can agree on, regardless of their party affiliation or where they are on the liberal/conservative spectrum. If these principles were to become major themes advanced in our congregations, from our pulpits and by believers, I am convinced that religion would make an important contribution to public discourse, and that we would go a long way toward mending broken politics. The four broad principles are these:

1. We should insist that politics remain in its proper place. It is not the realm of absolute truth and it is not the battleground of good and evil. Faithful people worship God. They do not worship political parties or ideologies. Certainly, politics is important and is worth doing well, but the exaggerated claims of politicians that their favored policies will miraculously solve our problems create exaggerated expectations, and per-

petually disappointed expectations create public cynicism. Against overwrought rhetoric of talking heads and radio personalities, our message should be, "Cool it." Our opponents are not our enemies.

2. We should be advocates for the common good. The framers of our Constitution were realistic in their understanding that politics consists of groups advancing their own interests, and they created a system of checks and balances to offset competing interests against one another. However, our first four presidents believed that the success of America would depend on citizens who did more than look after themselves. Besides promoting our own interests, it is important for Americans to advance the common good. Our early presidents called dedication to the common good "virtue." The concept of virtue was based on republican principles, not religion, and without a religious foundation it disappeared as a guiding principle for the nation. Today, politics consists of a competition of economic interests (more benefits or less taxes) plus ideologies largely reflecting those interests (more government or less government). Because the essence of religion is that the self is not the center of the universe, and because the model of Christianity is sacrificial love, religion can restore the lost principle that there is a higher good than the self.

3. We should be a unifying force, working to bind America together. One need only read the daily newspaper to know the power of religion to destroy countries; witness the violent confrontation of Sunni and Shiite Muslims in Iraq. Since our earliest days, Americans have been wary of how religion can divide us, and we have seen its divisive power at points in our history. But religion should have just the opposite effect. The words "religion" and "ligament" come from the same root meaning "to bind together." Jesus prayed for unity among his followers "that they may be one" (John 17:21), and the Epistle to the Colossians teaches that in Christ "all things hold together" (Colossians 1:17). Paul said that in Christ, God reconciled the world to himself, and entrusted to us the message of reconciliation (2 Corinthians 5:19). A fundamental premise of this book is that overcoming estrangement is the responsibility of faithful people and that God has entrusted us with the ministry of reconciliation. Because this is so, we should seek ways to make our ministry a practical reality.

4. We should advocate political compromise, and make the case that the spirit of compromise is consistent with our faith. There is tremendous pressure from party activists, media personalities, and interest groups for politicians to take uncompromising stands on is-

sues such as taxes and spending, but workable politics is the art of compromise, and the result of inflexible positions is gridlock. Faithful people, who do not think of politics in terms of absolutes, can be a counterpressure to those who pull politicians toward the ideological poles.

Focusing on the ministry of reconciliation helps us to see clearly the epicenter of broken politics and our role as a people in widening or healing that break. The epicenter is Congress where I served for eighteen years, that branch of government that in principle enables us to address our differences and live together, but in practice is dysfunctional.

When we think about the Constitution, our attention is usually on the first ten Amendments and their protections of our individual liberties. Those protections constitute an essential American value, but they aren't the totality of the Constitution. The body of the Constitution furthers a different and also essential value, that of holding together in one nation a diverse and often fractious people. That is why the Preamble begins with the words "We the people," as opposed to "I the individual." Directing our attention beyond the individual to our common life together is both an American and a religious enterprise. This value of creating one out of many was contested and finally upheld by the Civil War.

The principal mechanism the framers of the Constitution devised for holding together a diverse nation was Congress. It would be the branch of government most responsive to the variety of interests that made up America. Congress would be where we would advance our competing causes, find balance, and work out how to proceed as a nation. Congress would determine the federal government's policy on taxes, spending, war, and peace. For James Madison, the more interests engaged in making public policy the better. The aim wasn't that any interest would necessarily prevail on an issue, but that all would be heard, all would be welcome in the political process. If all would have the opportunity to participate in decision making, all would share allegiance to the structure that made their participation possible.

Today's controversies differ from those of the late eighteenth century. Slavery no longer divides us, and living in large or small states is of little matter. But we are now a much larger and more diverse country and our political controversies remain intense. The need for a functioning Congress is as great as ever, and therein lies the problem. Congress doesn't work. It isn't a place to present our causes and resolve our differences, so it isn't serving its constitutional purpose of holding America together.

Later, we will consider some institutional causes of Congress's dysfunction, including excessive use of the filibuster and unwillingness to vote on controversial issues. But the main culprit behind our broken government isn't the 535 members who serve in Washington; it's the public to whom the members respond. We are the culprits when we are so intent on getting our way and so certain of our ideology that we really don't want a structure where others are heard and differences are resolved, and we let our politicians know it. It is to us as citizens and to our intransigence that religion most powerfully speaks.

An obvious question is: Whose religion do I mean when discussing religion and politics? I am a Christian, and many of my references will perhaps have more meaning to Christian readers than to others. But my basic thoughts about the transcendence of God over politics, the centrality of the Love Commandment, and the role of religion in connecting us with one another are not uniquely Christian. Indeed, in my experience some of the people who have done the best job of living out the principles I suggest are Jews. So I hope that my own effort to work out the relevance of faith to politics will be helpful to citizens of different faiths as well as competing politics.

CHAPTER TWO

POLITICS IS NOT RELIGION

The goal of the ministry of reconciliation is to bind us together. Politics, when it functions as the Constitution provides, is the means of holding together a diverse nation. To that extent, there is overlap between the goal of religion and the practice of politics. But the two are very different realms, which was a lesson I learned in my 1982 reelection campaign for the Senate.

Toward the end of that campaign, I thought it was over. I had the desperate feeling that I was going to lose, as though my whole career was ending when I was only forty-six. In the month before election day, my opponent, Harriett Woods, had closed a fifteen-point gap and clearly had momentum on her side. I had cruised through my reelection campaign content with feel-good commercials, flattering myself that I had done a superb job in my first term as a U.S. senator, and convinced that my grateful constituents appreciated my service and would overwhelmingly return me to office. In a matter of hours, new polling numbers had turned my confidence into panic.

It wasn't just the sense that I was going to lose an election. I had done that before when, as a thirty-four-year-old challenger, I had nearly upset the revered three-term incumbent senator Stuart Symington. Then, losing wasn't so terrible, because few thought that I had any chance of winning, and many agreed that in retaining the office of state attorney general, I had a political future. This time it would be different. This time it would be the end. I was about to get the boot. In my mind's eye, hundreds of thousands of Missourians would set their alarm clocks and rush to the polls at daybreak for the express purpose of getting rid of me.

I ended up winning reelection by a narrow margin, but my anxiety was not lost on my family, which did its best to comfort me. Most memorable were the well-meaning words of my then fifteen-year-old daughter, D.D., who in the depths of my despair said matter-of-factly, "Well, it's not the World Series."

D.D.'s reassurance was touching and funny, and it also held a deeper meaning for me and, I hope, for all of us: It's important to keep politics in its proper place.

That autumn of 1982, my idea of politics lacked any sense of proportion. I started the campaign with a wildly exaggerated idea of what a marvelous job I had done in the Senate and how much I deserved the admiration of my constituents. Abruptly, this inflated self-esteem turned to the conviction that I would be humiliated and what made my life worthwhile was about to end. It was all about Jack. In hindsight, both my self-esteem and my self-pity seem so out of touch with reality as to be ridiculous.

Thankfully, even the most partisan political activists are not as wacky as I was during that long-ago campaign. Still, in our exuberance in victory and our despair in defeat, in our conviction that elections are momentous and that either deliverance is at hand or the end is near, our approach to politics can be overwrought.

It's important to keep things in perspective. Politics isn't the World Series. And politics certainly isn't religion. Religion can enrich politics, which should be the aim of faithful people. But politics and religion are different realms. Jesus made this clear when he answered whether it was lawful to pay taxes to the oppressive Roman Empire. Yes, he replied, people have a responsibility to support government by taxes, even to support the occupying power of Rome, but the things of Caesar are not the things of God. Politics isn't religion. We should remember this as we consider why politics can't replace religion and what religious people can bring to politics.

Politics is a mixture of principle and practicality, of public service and personal ambition. It calls for the considered judgment of officeholders and their dutiful attention to popular opinion, and it requires a balancing of conflicting interests of citizens. Its legislative work product is often excessively complex, with consequences that are usually uncertain and frequently unintended. At its best, politics can make life a little better; always it purports to do so; sometimes it does the opposite. Legislating is, as many have pointed out, like making sausage. It is messy, and what is messy may deserve our appreciation, but never our devotion.

Politics has gotten seriously off track because we, its practitioners, its activists, and its pundits, have pushed it there. We have turned it in a direction where it does not belong, a place of overblown promises and breathless alarm, of certainty that while there are two sides to every question, one side is absolutely right and the other is absolutely wrong. And we hold on to our notion of what is right with unshakable tenacity. Hence uncompromising politicians and bombastic commentators. Hence broken politics. If faithful people are to help fix broken politics, it is essential that we have a clear understanding of what politics is and that we offer America a clear statement of what it is not.

A famous description of politics at its best was given by British philosopher and statesman Edmund Burke in his 1774 "Speech to the Electors of Bristol at the Conclusion of the Poll." It answers a question frequently asked of me by high school students: "When you are in the Senate, do you vote your own conscience or the will of the people?" Burke wrote:

> It ought to be the happiness and glory of a representative to live in the strictest union, the closest correspondence, and the most unreserved communication with his constituents. Their wishes ought to have great weight with him; their opinion, high respect; their business, unremitted attention. It is his duty to sacrifice his repose, his pleasures, his satisfactions, to theirs; and above all, ever, and in all cases, to prefer their interest to his own. But his unbiased opinion, his mature judgment, his enlightened conscience, he ought not to sacrifice to you, to any man, or to any set of men living. These he does not derive from your pleasure; no, nor from the law and the constitution. They are a trust from Providence, for the abuse of which he is deeply answerable. Your representative owes you, not his industry only, but his judgment; and he betrays, instead of serving you, if he sacrifices it to your opinion.

Ultimately, for Burke, the people's representative must vote "his mature judgment, his enlightened conscience." At the same time, he must stay in "unreserved communication" with his constituents, and give their opinion "high respect." That, in essence, was my reply to the high school students. The relationship between a legislator and the people is dynamic. In the end, a senator should vote his or her conscience, otherwise why have representative democracy? Why have human beings holding public office? Why not weather vanes trying to catch the shifting drafts of popular sentiment? On the other hand, if a senator cared nothing about what the people think, convinced that he or she had all the answers, and didn't want to be bothered with other opinions, such a person, if elected once, would never be elected again. And shouldn't be. Not to mention what sort of personality disorder might give rise to such an inflated sense of one's own brilliance. The belief that "I'm right, everyone else is wrong" would ill equip one for the give-and-take of the legislative process.

An effective legislator must, as Burke said, be in touch with the electorate and respectful of their ideas. When it comes down to it, conscience trumps everything, but one's conscience should be tested against the will of the people. And when one's conscience dictates something different from the will of the people, the legislator owes the voters visits and explanations and more listening, and a readiness to face their wrath in the next election.

Burke interchangeably uses "conscience" and "judgment" to describe his priority as a legislator, indicating that he thinks it his duty to apply his best reasoning to his work rather than some perception of universal truth. Suppose a legislator votes contrary to strongly expressed public opinion, not on the basis of moral scruples, but because, on due consideration, he or she concludes that the popular approach would produce bad results. That, I thought, was the case during my first Senate term when we considered ratification of treaties that turned the Panama Canal over to its host country. Supporting the treaties was by far the most unpopular stand I took in my political career, triggering extremely hostile confrontations with enraged constituents that lasted not just during the several months when the treaties were considered by the Senate, but for years thereafter. Strong opposition to my position was statewide, and it was especially intense in some communities. Moberly comes to mind, where crowds that showed up for town hall meetings were furious to the point of being threatening. It seemed unimaginable to me that people could feel so strongly about a subject that before the treaties were negotiated had been dormant for decades. But for huge numbers of people, the canal, built during the presidency of Theodore Roosevelt, was a source of national pride. In the minds of canal enthusiasts, we (President Carter, the Senate, and I) were giving up national sovereignty to, as they put it, "a tinhorn dictator," President Torrijos of Panama.

I had no doubt that the treaties were in the best interest of the United States. After ratification, the canal would remain open to all nations, and we could continue to use it, as before, and on a priority basis in cases of emergency. The only difference would be that the chore of operating the canal would fall on the government of Panama. The treaties reminded me of Tom Sawyer getting someone else to paint a fence. More seriously, I foresaw endless trouble ahead if the United States continued to be the hated absentee proprietor of a fifty-mile-long structure highly vulnerable to terrorist attack. My vote was an easy decision on the merits, but a miserable decision because of the politics.

As Edmund Burke would have it, I used my best judgment, but contrary to Burke's advice, I sprang my position on my constituents without giving them an opportunity to express themselves. I had not been in "unreserved communication" with them, instead stating how I would vote as a fait accompli, and failing to give their opinion "high respect." My friend and fellow senator from Missouri, Tom Eagleton, immediately saw the blunder of my snap decision and was greatly amused by it, ever after greeting me as "Panama Jack." Of course, he ended up voting exactly as I did, but he gave our constituents the dignity of having their voices heard. All this is to say that the relationship between a legislator and the citizens is and should be dynamic. It is not a matter of the all-wise politicians handing down their wisdom to the ignorant public. In fact, politicians are not all-wise, and there is no reason that on questions of public policy the public should be ignorant.

But that is the assumption many people share. Any number of times during my Senate years, constituents would say, "Give us the inside scoop on what's happening in Washington. Out here, we don't know what's going on." The fact is that by taking the time to be informed, especially by reading a good newspaper, citizens can learn everything they could reasonably want to know on issues before the government. Many times, I attended top-secret briefings in the Senate Intelligence Committee, only to hear what I had already read in *The Washington Post.* If I as a senator knew more than my constituents, it was because it was my job to be informed, not because I had the inside scoop. Judgment has less to do with knowing esoteric facts than with acting on the facts you know. The day-to-day work of a legislator is to use judgment and test that judgment against the will of the people.

When measuring the will of the people, a politician will consider the intensity of feeling on one side of an issue more important than sheer numbers on the other side, because intensity determines active participation in campaigns, including financial support. This is why public opinion polls carry less weight with politicians than do positions taken by interest groups. Suppose two-thirds of poll respondents favor a certain measure, but not with sufficient ardor to influence their votes. On the same issue, 5 percent are so strongly opposed that they will vote against any candidate on the other side. In the calculation of the politician, the 5 percent will weigh more heavily than the two-thirds. This explains why single-issue voters can have a disproportionate effect on public policy. A good example is the National Rifle Association's successful opposition even to gun control legislation supported by strong majorities of people polled. Opponents of gun control will vote on that issue alone. Supporters will consider gun control but one of several issues. Thus members of Congress oppose gun control where the NRA holds the key to electoral success. Candidates are willing to accept mild opposition from large segments of their constituents. What they seek to avoid is enraging people they are counting on for support. My Senate friend John Chafee from Rhode Island often quoted Yale's famous football coach Herman Hickman on this point. Hickman said that it was his job to keep the Yale alumni "sullen but not rebellious."

In the final analysis, the way in which a politician measures the will of the people is quite simple. It isn't really a matter of reading the polls or weighing the mail. It's deciding how a position on an issue will affect the next election.

Here we have the third element of the dynamic of politics. The first is the politician's judgment of what is in the best interests of the country. The second is the will of the people against which the politician tests judgment. The third decides the issue when judgment and the will of the people are at odds: How badly does the politician want to win the next election? If a politician doesn't hold a strong opinion on an issue, a decision will not be difficult. A senator's judgment on an issue may be equivocal or lukewarm. One might think that on balance gun control legislation is a reasonable idea, but that it would do little good in reducing crime, so the senator might decide the issue in favor of the NRA. Or a senator may think that a vote before Congress, while a hot issue for some constituents, has little practical significance for public policy. Many times, senators vote on "sense of the Senate" resolutions that have no legislative effect but are important to someone. Despite reservations about the underlying issue, a senator may vote for such a resolution in order to please constituents, reasoning that the resolution is meaningless and does no practical harm.

The hard issues are the ones that have significance for the future of the country, and where the politician's decision is certain to enrage constituents. At the top of that list is, as it has been for decades, the future of Social Security and Medicare. Every politician has reached a judgment as to what must be done. Every such judgment is so intensely unpopular with huge segments of the electorate that it would determine the next election. Most politicians want to win the next election, so judgment gives way to public opinion. On these critical issues, the test of courage is to stand by one's judgment, even at the risk of electoral defeat.

The complexity of the legislative process can put the most courageous politician in the position of making difficult choices. In order to pass legislation, a bill's sponsor must accommodate the concerns of enough colleagues to win a majority of the votes. Usually this means adding, changing, or deleting provisions in a bill in order to make the legislation acceptable to persuadable colleagues. This process is popularly called "horse trading." The result is legislation that perfectly satisfies no one, but is close enough to be acceptable to the majority. A senator may end up voting for a bill on the basis of support for its overall content, even with strong objections to some of its parts. For example, I voted for final passage of anticrime legislation even though it expanded the use of the death penalty, which I opposed. Notwithstanding its objectionable provisions, I thought that the totality of the legislation was positive.

James Madison envisioned the legislative process as the balancing of competing interests, but Madison could not have imagined the abundance of competing interests in twenty-first-century America. In 2013, there were 9,434 registered lobbyists in Washington representing a multitude of different organizations that advocated an

infinite number of positions on every point of the ideological spectrum. Organizations include the U.S. Cham-
ber of Commerce, the AFL-CIO, television networks,
telephone companies, communication workers, environ-
mental groups, pro-life and pro-choice organizations, and
on and on. They endorse and oppose candidates, host
and attend political fund-raising events, conduct get-out-
the-vote efforts, and buy advertising. They are hyperatten-
tive to everything going on in government. The Senate
Finance Committee on which I served was a magnet for
lobbyists, leading Senator Bob Dole to call the hallway
outside the Committee Room "Gucci Gulch."

Because most legislation is the result of negotiation
and compromise, the result may not be a clear victory for
one side or the other. The Civil Rights Act of 1991 that I
authored overturned a number of restrictive Supreme
Court decisions on employment discrimination, and was
the product of months of intense negotiations with Senator Ted Kennedy on one side and the White House staff
of George H. W. Bush on the other. There were countless
arguments over precisely what words to use to describe
how an employer's job specifications would impact the
hiring of minorities and women. As might be expected of
a politician, I put out glowing press releases claiming that
my bill was the most important civil rights legislation to
pass Congress in more than a quarter century. But President Bush, who had opposed the bill, fearing that it

would create racial and gender quotas for employers to meet, also claimed victory, and signed the bill into law at a ceremony in the White House Rose Garden. The fact is that the claims of politicians about the importance of their work can be overblown. I thought that the 1991 act would have a positive effect on civil rights and that it would open opportunities for women and minorities. I certainly hope it has done that. A number of commentators say that the law encouraged more claims to be filed by both groups in the hopes of opening up opportunities. But in the more than two decades since its enactment, I have had no one tell me whether the increase in claims and cases following its passage actually resulted in more opportunity for the intended beneficiaries. The intellectual debate on this issue continues, but there does not seem to be any definitive answer. In fact, to this day, I don't know if the law had much of an effect one way or the other. Like many politicians, I supposed the country, and even the world, was waiting with rapt attention for the latest wonder to be produced by their representatives in government. In reality, despite the efforts of politicians, life goes on for constituents pretty much as it had before.

After awful tragedies, a mass shooting in a school or a terrorist attack, it's natural for the media to press politicians for answers: "What do you intend to do about school shootings?" The one unthinkable response is, "I have no idea what to do." So presidents appoint commissions, committees hold hearings, and congressmen introduce bills. A frequent comment is, "We must do [fill in the blank] so that this will not happen again." Governmental measures change in reaction to events. After a terrorist on an airplane tried to detonate his shoe, passengers were told to present their shoes for X-ray screening. However unlikely it may be that a future terrorist would use the same method again, no official wants to be blamed if it does happen, so off come the shoes.

Fixing yesterday's problem is a characteristic of government. Other characteristics are mind-boggling complexity and the creation of unintended consequences. Problems are big, government is big, and the complexity and degree of difficulty in effectively addressing problems seem to grow with the passage of years. When I was a law student, the Internal Revenue Code was a single volume the size of a large paperback book. Regulations under the code were printed in another single, much larger volume. Now the Internal Revenue Code covers 73,954 pages and the regulations take up twenty-five volumes. The Affordable Care Act is 961 pages, and the regulations under it currently exceed 10,000 pages.

Unintended consequences are the predictable result of complexity. The theory of the 1986 Tax Act was to pay for lower tax rates by reducing tax preferences that benefited specific segments of the economy. Before the 1986 act, commercial real estate had so benefited from generous deductions that most observers thought it only reasonable to let that business pay for a significant share of the new lower rates. However reasonable, the tighter rules were enacted precipitously, and were catastrophic to the commercial real estate business. Some experts believe the changes in the tax code contributed to the savings and loan crisis of the early 1990s.

The most dramatic example of bad results following good intentions is the recession that began in 2007. For commendable reasons, Congress and the executive branch believed that it would be good policy to bring homeownership within the reach of people with modest means. So government pressed banks to make subprime loans that homeowners could not afford. This contributed to the housing bubble that burst, leading to the Great Recession.

In sum, politics is a world of competing interests and trade-offs. Its focus is on the next election if not the next news cycle. It is often reactive and overly complex, and its consequences are uncertain and at times counterproductive. In none of these respects does it resemble religion.

The bargaining of Abraham with God over the future of Sodom (Genesis 18:17–33) is the closest biblical analogy I know between religion and politics, but even there, the difference is more striking than the similarity. Abraham begins by asking if God would destroy Sodom if there were fifty righteous people in the city, and eventually whittles the number down from fifty to ten. This sort of give-and-take is familiar in politics, but only to a point. The passage begins with God wondering out loud whether to tell Abraham what he intends to do with Sodom (Genesis 18:17). Unlike politics, where close contact with constituents is a requirement of success, God has the choice of bringing Abraham into the action or keeping him in the dark. By God's choice, Abraham is included, but Abraham knows his place, even when pushing against God: "Let me take it upon myself to speak to the Lord, I who am but dust and ashes" (Genesis 18:27). God creates humankind, comes into relationship with humankind, and shares his work with humankind (Genesis 1:28–31). But God is God, and we are only human.

The first political commission in the Bible is on Mount Horeb, where God instructs Moses to deliver the people of Israel from Egypt. When Moses turns toward the burning bush, God makes a point of keeping him in his place: "Come no closer! Remove the sandals from your feet, for the place on which you are standing is holy ground." Moses then asks God to tell him his name. To put it in slang terms, he asks God for a "handle." He wants a handle on God. God refuses such familiarity. "I am who I am" is the reply. The first difference, then, between religion and politics is that religion relates humankind to God, then as brothers and sisters to each other. Politics relates humans to humans. And while politics is often reactive, attempting to make sure that past events will never happen again, as with shoe bombers on planes, the covenantal relationship of religion looks to the future as with God's promise to Israel, "I am God Almighty: be fruitful and multiply; a nation and a company of nations shall come from you."

Unlike the legislative process, God's law does not reflect the will of the people. There are no focus groups, public opinion polls, or elections. The casting of the golden calf was an occasion of popular jubilation and revelry. When Moses came down from the mountain, people were shouting and dancing as if they were at a political convention. But the Ten Commandments, handed down from God with no public input, were the law. And unlike the thousands of pages of complexity produced by legislatures in order to satisfy competing interests and anticipate a variety of unintended consequences, the rules for living set out in the Bible are pithy and straightforward. Compare one verse from Saint Paul with 73,954 pages of the Internal Revenue Code: "For the whole law is summed up in a single commandment, 'You shall love your neighbor as yourself'" (Galatians 5:14).

There are two other important distinctions between religion and politics:

1. Politics is about power balanced among interests, and enforced by government. Religion is about a different kind of power, the work of God in our lives to bring about the kingdom (1 Corinthians 4:20). Christians follow the Lord, who "emptied himself, taking the form of a slave, being born in human likeness. And being found in human form, he humbled himself and became obedient to the point of death—even death on a cross" (Philippians 2:7–8). For Christians, sacrificing, losing, and dying are the conditions for resurrection.

2. Similarly, Madison's idea that a multitude of interests, ardently advanced by competing parties, are the basis for a just society stands in contrast with Paul's admonition:

> Do nothing from selfish ambition or conceit, but in humility regard others as better than yourselves. Let each of you look not to your own interests, but to the interests of others (Philippians 2:3–4).

The language of religion is strong, straightforward, uncompromising, and challenging. It puts us in our place, and it calls us to sacrifice. Whatever we might think of it, one thing should be clear. Politics is not religion, although we often act as though it were.

Twentieth-century theologian Paul Tillich described faith as the way in which we order our priorities. He said that faith is an expression of our "ultimate concern." We may have many interests, but we can only have one ultimate concern, which means that the question for religious people is whether our lives are centered in God or in something else. A non-churchgoing friend once told me that on Sunday mornings he worshipped God on the golf course. Maybe so; or maybe he worshipped golf on the golf course. Whichever it was, all of us worship either God or something else. A measure of our ultimate concern is how we devote our time and passion. It's chastening for the churchgoing political junkie (that would be me) to compare the hours we spend at worship and the hours we spend working ourselves into a lather watching twenty-four-hour news channels, because it's difficult to claim that God is our ultimate concern, the center of our being, when politics claims so much more of our time and our emotions.

When we do not keep politics in its proper place and when we make it our ultimate concern, when we turn politics into our religion, we transform it into something grotesque, and that is what we have done. "Grotesque" may seem a harsh word to use to describe the present state of American politics, but I think it is literally correct.

Its dictionary definition is "having the quality of ludicrous caricature or departing markedly from the natural, the expected, or the typical."* Fundamentally, politics is good, and it is essential to our democracy. By it, the people participate in the process of government. Through it, we can pursue not only our interests but our visions of a better society. But when we blow politics out of proportion and turn what is only approximate into what we claim is absolute, we make politics grotesque.

It would be good if we were to reorient our lives—the religious word is "repent"—if we were to spend more hours at worship and fewer in front of the TV, more time in prayer and less time in a rage. I do recommend that when pundits turn to wrath, we switch to something else. But I am realistic enough to know that as we live our lives I, and possibly you, will not in fact keep God as our ultimate concern. Other interests, including politics, will fill our days. We will not in reality love God with our whole heart. We will not in reality love our neighbor as ourselves. There is and will be a huge gulf between who we are supposed to be and who we are. Facing up to this gulf is the heart of confession, and when we face up to it, we put politics and everything else in perspective.

That's good for the soul. It's also good for the country. Because when we blow politics out of proportion, when we make it into something grotesque, it doesn't

* *Webster's Third New International Dictionary.*

work very well. It breaks down. And that is where we are today.

Religion and politics are separate realms that share the common goal of binding us together. Attaining this goal requires of both religion and state mutual respect, even deference.

The work of politics is to cobble the compromises needed to hold together more than three hundred million citizens and an infinite number of competing interests. This political work cannot succeed if government's policies don't bind everyone, and if religion's demands trump what government asks of all Americans. The constitutional provision that Congress cannot prohibit the free exercise of religion does not mean that religious people are exempt from generally applicable rules of law. As the Supreme Court has held, a religious doctrine that requires polygamy is not sufficient to protect its adherents from prosecution for a criminal offense.*

The principle that the law takes precedence over religious practice was articulated by Justice Antonin Scalia in a case deciding that a state could penalize two Native Americans for using peyote in a religious ceremony: "[The Court has] never held that an individual's religious beliefs excuse him from compliance with an otherwise

---

* *Reynolds v. United States,* 98 U.S. 145 (1878).

valid law prohibiting conduct that the State is free to regulate."* In earlier cases, the Supreme Court had held that government could build a road through a Native American sacred site,† and that the Air Force could forbid Jewish doctors from wearing yarmulkes while in uniform.‡

It does not follow from government's power to trump persons in the practice of their religions that it should always utilize that power. In particular, Congress has deferred to religious sensibilities by providing that members of the armed forces may wear religious apparel such as yarmulkes.§ More generally, Congress responded to Justice Scalia's opinion by enacting the Religious Freedom Restoration Act (RFRA), which provides that where a law is a substantial burden to the exercise of religion, the government must show that the law (a) is in furtherance of a compelling governmental interest, and (b) is the least restrictive means of furthering that interest.

In *Burwell v. Hobby Lobby Stores, Inc.*,¶ the Supreme Court held that government's requirement that religiously committed businesses insure employees for certain contraception methods did not meet RFRA's least

---

* *Employment Division v. Smith*, 494 U.S. 872 (1990).
† *Lyng v. Northwest Indian Cemetery Protective Association*, 485 U.S. 439 (1988).
‡ *Goldman v. Weinberger*, 475 U.S. 503 (1986).
§ National Defense Authorization Act of 1988.
¶ 573 U.S. ____ (2014), Docket no. 13-354.

restrictive means test. The Court pointed out that the government had created a less restrictive means of insuring employees of religious nonprofit organizations by shifting the cost of the coverage from employers to their insurance companies, and reasoned that this same means could be applied to for-profit corporations.

Although *Hobby Lobby* created a major political stir with various critics who claimed that the case would lead to wholesale avoidance of law and would result in employers imposing their own religious beliefs on employees, its effect is far less sweeping. *Hobby Lobby* was decided by applying a federal statute, not by interpreting the Constitution. Had the Constitution been determinative, the case would most likely have turned out the other way, and would have followed Scalia's opinion in holding that "an individual's religious beliefs [do not] excuse him from compliance with an otherwise valid law." Far from recognizing an exemption from the mandate as a right, the Court described it as "an accommodation." If the government chooses, it can accommodate the religious concerns of employers, but the Constitution doesn't require government to do so.

The least restrictive means test applied by the Supreme Court in *Hobby Lobby* goes only to the question of who pays for the contraceptive methods at issue, the employer or the insurance company. In either case, the end would be the same, and exactly the same insurance coverage would be extended to the employees. As the Court stated, "The effect of the HHS-created accommodation on the women employed by Hobby Lobby and the other companies involved in these cases would be precisely zero."

In *Hobby Lobby*, the Supreme Court assumed that government has "a compelling interest" to mandate insurance coverage for contraception, including coverage for the four methods the employers found objectionable on religious grounds. Notwithstanding such objections, the Constitution would not prevent the government from requiring employers to pay for such coverage if the government so chose. But in RFRA, Congress created a least-restrictive-means test, and in its "accommodation" to religious nonprofit organizations, government created a less restrictive means that could be applied to for-profit businesses. In sum, government has broad power to exert itself over religious objections. The real question is whether government, and ultimately the American people, want to exercise that power, and if so, when. Should the military forbid Jews from wearing yarmulkes? Should a highway run through an Indian burial ground if another route is available? Should Catholic hospitals be forced to pay for abortions if the cost can be borne by insurance companies? America's current policy is for government to accommodate religious concerns where it can accomplish its objectives by other means.

RFRA was noncontroversial when it was enacted in 1993. The vote in the Senate was 97–3, and it was approved by voice vote in the House of Representatives. I have no doubt that its principles are widely shared by the American people today, despite the outcry over *Hobby Lobby*. While under Supreme Court decisions government has the power to override even the strongly held religious objections of faithful people, it should honor religious sensibilities when it can, and make every effort to coexist with religion. But how about religion coexisting with politics? Religious people can influence both the tone of politics and, by their votes and advocacy, the content of public policy. An important question is when, in addressing politics, they should use the prophetic voice. The work of prophets, in the Old Testament tradition, is to express their understanding of God's commands in unequivocal terms, often by openly confronting political power. As I shall argue later, use of the prophetic voice is the responsibility of the faithful when calling America to turn from the single-minded political focus on serving self-interest toward a religiously inspired commitment to the common good. However, as a general rule, speaking righteously in the name of God is not appropriate when advocating specific political agendas.

There are exceptions, but they are rare in the real world of contemporary American politics. Where evil exists—slavery and Nazism being historic examples—

prophets must speak out against government. But suppose a situation far short of evil. Suppose merely competing interests and differing opinions. That is America today: a good country with a lot of good people who disagree with each other on a lot of issues. When good-faith differences of opinion exist, the prophetic approach to issues doesn't speak for God but uses God to advance a point of view. Then the prophetic approach is worse than out of place—it is destructive of the civility that holds us together. So while the prophetic voice is essential in the appropriate time and place, the better ministry in America today is reconciliation that aims to hold us together with all our differences.

Even when faithful people are convinced that they speak for God against what they strongly believe is evil, there are circumstances in which it is well to step away from political fights and advance their causes in nonpolitical forums. These circumstances exist when the issues involved are highly divisive and the chance of changing public policy by legislative action is close to zero. The specific issues that meet this description are abortion and same-sex marriage.

When suggesting alternatives to politics, it's important to make two points. First, I am not arguing that as a general rule faithful people should bypass politics and seek other routes to their objectives. Religion is relevant to all of life, particularly politics, and religious people should be more engaged in politics if their hope is to heal it. I am saying that there are a few issues where politics is not the best forum to advance a cause, and we would be well advised to direct our attention elsewhere. The second point is an acknowledgment that it is a very tough sell to persuade religious people to turn from politics when the issues at stake are, for them, critically important. Values they hold dear have been affected by governmental actions, especially by decisions of the Supreme Court, so it's understandable that they look to government as the source of redress. Also, as a practical matter, it's easier to focus the public on an issue by concentrating attention on a specific legislative proposal, even if enactment is hopeless, than by making an amorphous statement on a philosophical generality.

Where big and highly contentious social issues are at stake—abortion and gay marriage are the most prominent—it is natural for the competing sides to want to win the most decisive possible victories over their opponents. This is especially true when activists believe that their cause concerns fundamental moral values that are at the heart of their religious faith. In those cases, partial success will not satisfy the advocates. They will not compromise on matters of principle.

The most sweeping way to win a moral issue is to have one's position written into the Constitution, an objective far more easily accomplished by Supreme Court decision than by the almost impossibly difficult route of constitutional amendment. This is why the federal courts have been the favorite place to wage our culture wars. Jurists and scholars disagree on whether and when disputed questions of societal values graduate from the political forum to constitutional principles. Whatever the point, the Supreme Court has claimed the authority to take matters out of the hands of legislatures. As far as public policy is concerned, when the Supreme Court decides that an issue is constitutional, it seldom matters what the losing side thinks. It is possible that over a very long span of time the Supreme Court may change its mind and adapt its position to changing times, as it did in *Brown v. Board of Education,* but for the foreseeable future, public policy is fixed. The losers can complain in blogs and editorials or in their pulpits, but they are shouting into the wind.

When the Supreme Court decides that a moral question is a constitutional right, the predictable response of the losing side is not to concede defeat and to keep fighting. For them the issue remains of critical, often religiously inspired significance. Refusing to quit, they search for every possible way to lessen their loss. They mobilize efforts in state legislatures to pass new laws that might salvage something for their cause. Recently in Texas there has been an effort to reduce to twenty weeks the age of the fetus when legal abortions can be performed.

Shortly after the Supreme Court decided *Roe v. Wade*, the Missouri General Assembly passed a new law with the intention of being as restrictive on abortions as possible without crossing the line the Supreme Court had drawn. As state attorney general, I defended the new law in federal district court and then, unsuccessfully, in the Supreme Court. But the Missouri effort could not have overturned the Supreme Court. It would have done little more than require parental or spousal consent and disallow a specific method of second-term abortions. In short, it was a rearguard action, and it failed.

Given the Supreme Court precedent now in place for four decades, there is little chance that a fresh assault on *Roe v. Wade* will prevail in court, even if it is successful in state legislatures. As a matter of law, legal abortion will remain with us. I have no doubt that the same will be true with regard to same-sex marriages. Legal victories by opponents, if any, will be few and at the margins, so what is the purpose of fighting political battles once the war has been lost in the Supreme Court? Even more, what is the point of fighting such battles after the Court's decisions have been widely accepted by the public?

There is certainly some advantage for advocacy groups that can raise funds and retain staff by going through the motions of keeping an issue alive. But as a pro-life Republican with a traditional view of marriage, I am convinced that fighting for lost causes is a political disaster. The heart of Republican ideology is confidence in the private sector, conservatism about the cost and power of government, and support for an engaged foreign policy and a strong national defense. With attractive candidates, these have been and should be winning positions. But in recent election cycles, my party has applied litmus tests on social issues to our candidates, forcing them into untenable positions as the price of winning nominations. The result has been candidates like Christine O'Donnell and Todd Akin who have no chance of winning general elections.

That politics is not a promising forum for pro-life advocates and supporters of traditional marriage to fight for their strongly held principles does not mean that there is nowhere else for them to press their positions. It is not true that government is the sole decider of moral questions. When controversies are cultural, the most likely way to win one's point is to change the culture, and changing the culture is precisely the mission of churches and their members. Pro-life advocates often say that the real problem they face is larger than abortion, it is the devaluation of life, what they call the "culture of death." Opponents of same-sex marriage say that their real aim is to defend the institution of marriage, and they point out that half the marriages in the United States end in divorce. By working in society as a whole, not just in politics, there is plenty of room to change the culture.

One of the finest people I was privileged to know in my political life was the leading pro-life advocate in our state, Loretto Wagner. A woman of deep Catholic faith, she served as president of Missouri Citizens for Life, and dedicated herself to overturning the effects of *Roe v. Wade.* Loretto's energetic efforts did not change the law and the Supreme Court's decision is still with us, but she has had a great effect on the culture of Missouri.

This began when B. J. Isaacson-Jones, who at the time was director of Missouri's largest abortion clinic, requested a meeting of pro-choice and pro-life leaders to discuss shared interests such as preventing unwanted pregnancies. The initial meeting led to monthly dinners and the creation of an informal group the participants called "Common Ground." As Loretto Wagner describes the dinners, "We talked for hours. We talked about our families and really became friends. I never thought I would be able to say that. We realized that these are human beings with feelings. A magical thing happened between all of us." The new friendships created what Loretto calls "an atmosphere of trust" in which participants could discuss their differences in a civil manner. Positive results followed. Isaacson-Jones called Loretto about a ten-year-old who initially came to the clinic for an abortion, only to decide to keep the baby. Since the girl had a complicated pregnancy, Isaacson-Jones asked Loretto to find a caregiver to look after the girl while her mother was at work. Loretto raised money to pay for the caregiver. The baby was subsequently put up for adoption. The Common Ground partners worked together to support state legislation to pay for pregnant drug addicts. The abortion clinic opened on-premises adoption services to provide an alternative to unwanted pregnancies. In the grand scheme of the long raging debate over abortion, none of these achievements were earthshaking, but each showed that people who seek common ground can find it, and in finding it they can change the culture of a community.

Saint Paul looked to the community rather than the law to enforce proper conduct. Writing to the Corinthians, he condemned a range of misconduct beginning with sexual immorality and including idolatry and robbery (1 Corinthians 5:19). What's most interesting in this passage is the choice of remedy Paul selects for confronting misconduct. He says that Christians should not take other Christians to court; that is, they should not avail themselves of the laws of the state to enforce the demands of proper behavior. Instead, Paul says that Christians should disassociate themselves from their immoral brethren. "Do not even eat with such a one," he advises. Shunning bad actors seems a harsh remedy in light of a Lord who ate with tax collectors and prostitutes, but Paul's broader point is that what God requires of his people is better enforced by the norms of the community than by the laws of the state. This is especially so when the demands of the faith are greater than the requirements of the state. The idolatry Paul lists as an offense was not a violation of Roman law. Similarly, when Jesus equated insults with murder and lust with adultery (Matthew 5:22, 28), the standards in the Gospel were far more demanding than what government could encapsulate in law. For Paul, standards enforced by other Christians compel moral conduct.

British political philosopher Danny Kruger describes "social authority" as "the set of encouragements and admonitions which operate in settled neighborhoods and among people who trust each other."* In other words, behavioral controls can come from sources other than the law. They can come from social approval or disapproval. A story my sister told about her childhood illustrates the point. Responding to a classmate who feared being "grounded" for some infraction of family rules, my sister recalled that once when she had done something bad our father had quietly said, "Dotty, I'm disappointed in you." My sister told her friend that she would rather be grounded for months than ever again hear our father say he was disappointed in her. Most of us spend little time worrying that if we don't behave ourselves the authorities will catch us and haul us into court. For most of us, com-

* Danny Kruger, *On Fraternity: Politics Beyond Liberty and Equality* (London: Civitas: Institute for the Study of Civil Society, 2007), 56.

plying with the minimal standards the state imposes on us is a matter of course. What we strive for is the approval of those whose respect we seek. What we try to avoid is their disapproval. An obvious place to learn what is required of people who live good lives is our churches. This means that a church that wants to change the culture has to stand for something. It would not be enough for a church to convey the message that as you live your life anything goes because all is forgiven.

Religious people who want to fix broken politics should participate actively in it, but they should try to make politics better, not worse. Where their political activity is far more divisive than promising, there are other, better ways to be agents of change. When they cannot change government, they may be able to change culture.

CHAPTER THREE

THE MAKING OF VIRTUOUS CITIZENS

For our founders, the future of America would depend on the virtue of its citizens. If the nation was to succeed, we would have to put the good of the whole above the interests of ourselves. The question, then, is what moves us to be virtuous, what causes us to live not only for our own sakes but also for the good of others? In part, it's how we are made. Each of us is some combination of nature and nurture, how we are born and how our environment affects who we become. How we are born is the given. How we develop depends on what we learn, the values we are taught, and the behavior we observe in people around us.

Religion is the most persistent and effective teacher of virtue, because living beyond ourselves, for God and neighbor, is the heart of its message. The ethos of politics is quite the opposite: It's all about us. As stated in the 1950s, "What's good for General Motors is good for America." Whether we are pulled toward virtue or in the opposite direction depends on the company we keep. Consider, for example, a night at the ballpark.

In a lifetime of attending St. Louis Cardinals games, I recall only one really miserable experience, so miserable that I have thought about it many times since, wondering about the reasons that accounted for it. Of course, I am not including the ordinary losses in sports under the heading "miserable." Watching my home team be swept by the Red Sox in the 2004 World Series was disappointing, but it was not an experience that recurs in my mind, causing me to wonder how it could be, how someone could have behaved that way, how I could have responded that way.

We sometimes read of melees in European soccer stadiums and isolated violence to visiting fans in the United States, but never in St. Louis. Cardinals fans are numerous, attentive, loud, colorful, and, with few exceptions, a joy to be with. By colorful, I mean both in the bright red outfits nearly everyone wears and in the characters who have populated the team's history. In my childhood, there was Mary Ott, "the Pig Lady," who sat in the lower deck on the first-base side and emitted ear-piercing squeals, and "Wingy," a man with a Cardinal tattoo on the stump of his amputated arm, who set the bird in circular flight when the team rallied. In recent years, a joyful man in modified Uncle Sam attire has stationed himself on the corner of Broadway and Market Streets with a sign,

"Welcome Cubs Fans." All of this has been for me a lifetime of fun, although as my wife, Sally, will attest, extreme anxiety when things aren't going well. I say this to make clear that the miserable event I will now describe was for me singular, although a somewhat related incident, which I will discuss later, was reported by another fan.

The miserable event happened maybe a dozen years ago when Sally and I, with our adult son, Tom, were seated in the lower deck of Busch Stadium on the third-base side. Immediately behind Sally, in the next row, was a man who appeared to be in his early twenties and his woman companion of about the same age. Early in the game, before his copious intake of beer had a chance to take hold, the young man dropped the f-bomb. It wasn't a soft, muted explosion. It was a jarring report that could be heard for rows around. And it wasn't an isolated, surgically targeted, cruise missile–like attack, a single word dropped once for dramatic or hoped-for comic effect and then forgotten. No, it went on and on, inning after inning, loudly and in every imaginable grammatical form: verb, noun, adjective, gerund. Every sentence from the young man's always-open mouth included it, sometimes several times. It was f-carpet bombing.

I do not want you to think that I am an exceptionally prudish person, the Reverend Goody-Goody, whose delicate ears must be protected from the sort of language most people hear at some point nearly every day. That absolutely does not describe me. But this was so loud, so unremitting, so over the top that it has a unique place in the memory of one who has heard it all. And I wish I could tell you that I handled the situation in some appropriate manner. Certainly I wanted the man to stop, and I could have asked him to do so. I didn't, perhaps out of fear. I could have asked an usher to intervene. Ushers have the power to confront obnoxious fans and, if necessary, remove them. I didn't do that either. Instead, and to my embarrassment, I, in the presence of my wife and son, turned in my seat and dropped the f-bomb back on him. I only did it once, but once is disgraceful enough, and of course it had zero effect. I have been thinking about that evening ever since, and what it says about that young man, and about me, and about the times in which we live.

It's impossible to put one's self in the mind of another person, especially when that person is a stranger, but it's possible to speculate why the young man thought it was okay to act the way he did. It was as though he was unaware that other people were around to hear him. But of course he was aware. He was in a baseball stadium with thirty or forty thousand people, some of whom were only a few feet from him, and he was loud. My wife, sitting directly in front of him, was old enough to be his mother, maybe his grandmother. He knew that. It's unimaginable that he would have acted that way in the presence of his mother or grandmother. But then he may have thought that this older lady in front of him wasn't his mother or grandmother. He may have thought that if his circle of concern included anyone other than himself, it was limited to very few people, maybe only close relatives. In this manner of thinking, no one else counted. Everyone else was in some lesser category, some place of little value, maybe not even a place of people. Maybe a place of things.

I once spoke with a physician who had served in combat, attending to badly wounded military personnel. Since he was not a surgeon by training, but had to act as one in battle, I asked how it was possible to attend to horribly mangled bodies. He said that he had to will himself to treat wounds as though they were objects detached from human beings. This was an act of will, born of the necessity to save lives. But for the young man at the ball game, there was no necessity, no good purpose served, no act of will. It may be that there was simply no belief that the people near him were worth his concern.

Or it could be that the young man wasn't oblivious to the rest of us as human beings with sensitivities. Perhaps he was fully aware of us and how we felt, and wanted to use us for his own purposes. He might have been on a power trip, showing off his ability to say anything at any place. His perception of our weakness may have given him a sense of strength.

Whatever the case, his were clearly acts of isolation, one man in a crowd intentionally setting himself apart from others. As such, it was an example of the disconnectedness many people feel from society, which we shall discuss later. But in a different way, the young man's conduct did relate to the world beyond himself. He may well have thought that what he was saying was perfectly permissible because it was no different from what he heard around him every day. He may have thought that his manner of speaking was part of his culture. Sadly, he would have been correct. It was and is part of his culture.

The offensive word in question has been around for a very long time, but it has mostly been used in private, not broadcast to the world. I have a clear memory of where I first heard it in a film. It was in a movie theater on Palmer Square in Princeton, New Jersey, so I was college age. Whatever the movie, the word was used once, and the moment went by so quickly and so surprisingly that I wondered if I had heard it. Now, half a century later, it's difficult to find any movie that does not use the word, often many times over, and usually in ways that add nothing to the artistic content of the film. That's just movies. Then there's hip-hop music and late-night "comedy" shows on TV. The entertainment industry has transformed a verbal aside into standard cultural fare.

I add a thought about my own conduct during that

evening at the ballpark, and I'm not speaking of my ridiculous foray into the land of obscenity. Absent that little fillip, my answer to inning after inning of outrage was to do nothing at all. I sat there and took it, and by my inaction, I allowed others to take it as well. In short, I took no responsibility for changing what was happening. Colleges that have honor systems—and I attended one—stress the importance of both the integrity of the individual and the integrity of the system itself. Before matriculating, students had to write in their own words their understanding of what would be required of them. The requirement had two parts. Students were not to cheat, and they were to turn in anyone who did cheat. On completing an exam, each student was required to write and sign a pledge: "I pledge my honor as a gentleman [it was at the time an all-male college] that I have neither given nor received information during this examination." As part of the arrangement, the professor who taught the course would leave the room after passing out the questions, and the room would be unproctored. The honor system was an essential component of my college experience.

The pledge we signed after completing exams promised only that each student had not cheated, but the part about turning in known cheaters, agreed to in writing before matriculation, was clearly understood. For the system to work, it required honorable conduct by individuals and zero tolerance for violations. We were responsible for both ourselves and the whole.

That, I believe, is the nature of being a responsible member of a society. We are more than an atomized assortment of individuals who are concerned solely about our personal behavior. Our sphere of responsibility extends to what goes on around us, our neighbors, our community, our nation, our world. For religious people, especially for those who take seriously the parable of the Good Samaritan, that sphere of responsibility is comprehensive indeed. The behavior of the oafish young man at the ball game still troubles me. So does my willingness to do nothing.

In their book *Switch*, Chip and Dan Heath discuss the contagious nature of human behavior. We pick up cues as to what other people are doing, and we act accordingly. This, they say, goes for tipping. Bartenders "seed" tip jars to tell us that others have left tips, so we are expected to do so. Tip containers are visible on Starbucks counters. On the other hand, say the Heaths, we don't tip baggers in grocery stores, because there is no indication that others do. That baggers do at least as much for us as Starbucks employees doesn't enter the picture. The Heaths present other intriguing examples of giving and receiving cues for how we are expected to behave: TV sitcom producers supply soundtracks of laughter to cue us when we are supposed to laugh; we use the phrase "at the end of the day" because we have heard others use it.*

We Americans believe that we can change everything by changing the law, when more consequential change comes from our behavior. What we do affects what other people do, and visa versa. We can influence people for good as with acts of kindness or for ill, which we shall consider shortly, or, as in the use of "at the end of the day," in ways that are morally neutral. But if we are in the least visible to other people, our actions do have consequences beyond ourselves. Some of the things we do, even if we think that they are for purely private satisfaction, harm others. Consider, for example, violence in the media.

I enjoy action-packed movies as much as the next guy, although no doubt much that is out there is too grisly for my taste. The entertainment industry makes products in order to sell them. When movies or TV shows bomb, they don't last. So when I watch a movie, I could claim that I am in my own private world, in my home or in a darkened theater, and that I have every right to enjoy myself in privacy. As a legal matter, that is correct. I have a right to watch the show of my choice, just as its producer has a right to make it. But in paying to see the show, I am sup-

* Chip Heath and Dan Heath, *Switch: How to Change Things When Change Is Hard* (New York: Broadway Books, 2010), chapter 10.

porting it financially and creating a culture that demands it. So it is not correct to say that my choices in entertainment are solely my private affair. My choice of personal entertainment affects other people, and in the case of violent entertainment it affects children.

A report of the American Academy of Pediatrics begins, "Exposure to violence in media, including television, movies, music, and video games, represents a significant risk to the health of children and adolescents." The report states, "The evidence is now clear and convincing: media violence is one of the causal factors of real-life violence and aggression."[*]

I am not advocating censorship or some other governmental policy to remedy the problem of violence in the media. Indeed, because of the First Amendment, this is a perfect example of one of my themes—the limitations of what government can accomplish. If we are to change the culture, it will not be because government can somehow do that for us. It will be because we decide by our own marketplace decisions to change the culture.

The most important of all personal decisions—with whom we choose to live our lives—has the most dramatic effect on our children. In 1960, 9 percent of American children lived in single-parent homes. Half a century later, that percentage had more than tripled to 29.5 per-

---

[*] "Media Violence," *Pediatrics* 124, no. 5 (November 1, 2009).

cent.* According to sociologist Sara McLanahan, a single-parent family, after adjusting for all other factors such as race and gender, has a dramatic effect on child welfare, decreasing family income by 40 percent by age seventeen while the income of two-parent families grew 8.5 percent, and doubling the high school dropout rate.† A child born into a fatherless home is three times more likely to be incarcerated by age thirty than a child who grew up in a two-parent home.‡ As with media violence, I am not recommending government action, only pointing out that the notion that our personal choices affect only ourselves is simply not true.

The Holocaust is among the darkest epochs in human history, and serves as a grim reminder of group behavior at its worst.§ Elie Wiesel describes starkly his own dreadful experience, capturing the blackness of the era in his

* U.S. Bureau of the Census, *Living Arrangements of Children Under 18 Years Old: 1960–Present* (September 15, 2004), and U.S. Bureau of Labor Statistics, updated and revised from "Families and Work in Transition in 12 Countries, 1980–2001," *Monthly Labor Review* (September 2003).

† Sara McLanahan, "Father Absence and the Welfare of Children," in *Coping with Divorce, Single Parenting and Remarriage: A Risk and Resiliency Perspective,* ed. E. Mavis Hetherington (Mahwah, NJ: Lawrence Erlbaum Associates, 1999), 117–45.

‡ Cynthia C. Harper and Sara S. McLanahan, "Father Absence and Youth Incarceration," *Journal of Research on Adolescence* (2004): 369–97.

§ The following paragraphs draw on sermons I preached at the Washington National Cathedral on April 29, 1979, and April 18, 1993, and on remarks I delivered at the United States Holocaust Museum on May 24, 1994.

book's title, *Night*. That it was. In the end, Nazis murdered six million Jews, one million of whom were children. Nearly 90 percent of the Jewish population of Poland was exterminated. Because the Holocaust occurred at a distant time on a distant continent, because Adolf Hitler was so singularly demonic, because the scale of the carnage was so immense, one could say that it has no relevance to the United States, and that we should remember it simply as we memorialize any past event. But human beings of the early twenty-first century do resemble human beings of the twentieth century, which is why the Holocaust is of more than historical significance. How could people have been part of this? How could they have allowed it to happen to other humans? How could they have actively participated in it? And of direct interest to us now and for all times, what is our responsibility to other people, just because they are human?

The common excuse given by the German people after World War II was that they should not be held responsible because they didn't know what was going on. It was someone else's fault, not theirs. In the parable of the Good Samaritan, why should the priest and the Levite not pass by on the other side if they don't notice a man lying by the side of the road? We use the same excuse today. We say we don't know what's happening around us. It's someone else's job. It's none of our business. It is an excuse so preposterous that it cannot be explained by willful neglect. It is for us, as it was for Germans of the mid-twentieth century, a lie.

But of course, ordinary Germans did know what was happening. The Holocaust wasn't a passing event undertaken by a small number of insiders. It was an enormous enterprise that spanned twelve years. Ordinary Germans could not have missed the burning of synagogues and the pillaging of Jewish shops in the 1930s. Hitler's anti-Jewish rants before massive crowds were meant for their ears. They could not have missed the Gestapo rounding up their neighbors and cattle cars filled with Jews criss-crossing their country. Killing Jews wasn't some secondary concern of Nazi officials; it assumed greater priority than fighting the war. Trains carrying Jews to concentration camps were more important than trains carrying ammunition to the front. Consider how many people it would take to round up six million Jews and transport them to death camps. Consider how many people built and manned the camps and supervised forced labor. Every sentient person in Germany participated in or knew about the Holocaust. The claim that they didn't know and therefore were not responsible is simply false.

It's especially troubling to know that Germany in the 1930s and 1940s was a nation of long Christian tradition, both Catholic and Lutheran. While a few Christians, notably Dietrich Bonhoeffer, witnessed against the Nazi regime to the point of martyrdom, many who actively participated in or passively consented to the Holocaust were Christians. The Jewish Historical Museum in Holland has a photograph of SS officers celebrating Christmas in a concentration camp.

Our sense of responsibility is sharpened when we think not about abstractions but about particularities. It can overwhelm our capacity to grasp the horror of events if we think only of a long duration and a large number and complicated logistics. The Holocaust was a crime against humanity, but crimes against humanity are not generalities. They are not abstractions, but acts committed against individuals, each with his own identity, his own history, his own dignity. The experience of visiting the United States Holocaust Memorial Museum in Washington, D.C., is so powerful that it numbs the senses. So it's important to have some focus and give one exhibit concentrated attention. The exhibit that riveted my attention when I saw it twenty years ago and that haunts me today was on the third floor of the museum on a television screen describing medical experiments. It was a series of four photographs of a dwarf, a Dutch Jew named Alexander Kalan. The sequence of photographs showed Kalan first face-on and dressed in prison clothes, then face-on and naked, then in profile and naked; finally, his skeleton. The legend beneath the pictures explained that prison personnel at Mauthausen stabbed him to death so that scientists could study his skeleton.

What was striking about the photographs was their particularity. They were of one man, in isolation. No one was with him. Nothing was in the background. They were photographs of Alexander Kalan and nothing else, stripped first of his personhood, then of his clothing; finally of his flesh. These photographs told me that as the Holocaust claimed six million lives, each person was unique. The Holocaust proceeded one arrest at a time, one internment at a time, one experiment at a time, one shooting at a time, one gassing at a time. Our responsibility is to humanity, an abstraction, but more concretely, it is to each individual.

Particularity is important when we consider the perpetrators as well as the victims. In his disturbing book *Ordinary Men,** Christopher Browning studies a reserve police battalion of five hundred Germans who during Hitler's regime had the job of ridding Poland of Jews. They did their work with rifles, leading women, children, and those men too weak for work into the woods, forcing them to lie prone, and shooting them in the base of the skull. One at a time, these five hundred men murdered thirty-eight thousand Jews.

Each police officer could have avoided participating in the shooting without penalty. Just before they began the first day of their work, their commanding officer an-

* Christopher R. Browning, *Ordinary Men: Reserve Police Battalion 101 and the Final Solution in Poland* (New York: HarperPerennial, 1992).

nounced that any policemen who didn't have the stomach for it would be excused, and that remained the standing offer for the next two years. Even though many participants were sickened by what they were doing, only about a dozen men stepped out that first day, and only 15–20 percent declined to participate as the slaughter continued. Those who declined were not punished.

Browning offers a multicausal explanation of why ordinary men would do this, including deference to authority, racism, and the effects of war, but he singles out for special attention "the pressure for conformity—the basic identification of men in uniform with their comrades and the strong urge not to separate themselves from the group by stepping out."

We have the power to take responsibility for our actions. We have the power to say, "I won't do it," or even to say, "Stop it!" What others do influences us. Conversely, what we do influences others. Taking responsibility for ourselves and for our neighbors is our religious obligation.

One way to avoid responsibility for the world in which we live is to plead ignorance. Another is to place blame elsewhere. This is the tactic of conspiracy theorists. Conspiracy theories purport to identify causes of events and grievances, and are of ancient origin. Criminal law provides for the prosecution of conspiracies, that is, acts performed by more than one individual. Conspiracies do exist. For example, the Watergate break-in was a conspiracy, because it involved several people. By contrast, conspiracy theorists imagine dark forces that do not exist, and engage in demonization. Conspiracy theories were common in the Middle Ages, especially those directed at Jews, who were accused of killing Jesus and consuming Christian blood in rituals. In the late nineteenth century, Jews and Freemasons were accused of plotting to control the world. Recently, anti-Semitism has focused on alleged Jewish control of the financial system and Hollywood. Modern conspiracy theories have developed after the assassinations of President Kennedy and Martin Luther King Jr. and the death of Princess Diana. They purport to explain the spread of HIV/AIDS, and they allege that various secretive and powerful groups are attempting to establish a New World Order, or have succeeded in doing so. The accused organizations include the Trilateral Commission, the Bilderberg Group, and the World Bank. The implication is that ordinary citizens are helpless victims, and matters are out of their hands because sinister forces are at work.

The more sophisticated and ubiquitous the media, the more convincing and publicly accessible the theories. YouTube is an especially effective medium, featuring among other offerings a documentary with interviews of alleged engineering experts claiming to show that the destruction of the twin towers on 9/11 was an inside job.

My personal experience with a conspiracy theory was a consequence of the 1993 disaster at the Branch Davidian religious compound near Waco, Texas. The facts were that four federal agents of the Bureau of Alcohol, Tobacco and Firearms were shot to death and others were injured while trying to serve a search warrant. Then followed a fifty-one-day standoff when FBI agents surrounding the compound unsuccessfully tried to persuade the Branch Davidians to surrender. Finally, the FBI inserted tear gas, and people inside the building directed gunfire at the agents. A fire broke out and more gunfire ensued. In the end, at least eighty Branch Davidians, including children, died of gunshots or by fire. Thereafter, a very persuasive and widely viewed documentary appeared that made the case that FBI agents had directed gunfire into the building and ignited the fire. On August 26, 1999, a poll printed in *Time* magazine indicated that 61 percent of the public believed that federal law enforcement officials started the fire. Attorney General Janet Reno appointed me special counsel to determine whether the allegations were true.

Within a few months of commencing the investigation it was clear to me and to everyone helping with the investigation that there was no basis for suspicions that government agents had committed bad acts. In an ordinary lawsuit where a court could have determined the facts by the weight of the evidence, we could have wrapped up the matter in short order. But this wasn't an ordinary lawsuit. It wasn't enough for us to weigh the evidence; we had to exhaust the evidence, laboriously running down every conceivable possibility and repeatedly testing every conclusion.

A difficulty with conspiracy theories is that it is very hard to prove a negative. If someone asserts that extraterrestrial beings are among us, how does one prove that they are not? There is no presumption of innocence of the accused. All the theorist has to do is make an accusation that is plausible and the burden shifts to the accused to disprove it. In the Waco investigation, we knew that if we left any detail unexplored, the theorists would pounce on it as proof that we had failed to do our job. More than that, by debunking the theory we would be open to the charge that we were part of the conspiracy.

The investigation of the Waco disaster lasted fourteen months and cost $17 million. We convened a grand jury, retained experts, and staged a recreation of gunfire at Fort Hood, Texas. At the end, we went through our draft report page by page to give our investigators a final opportunity to raise any possible questions. The result was that everyone who participated in the investigation agreed with every detail of our findings. The shooting deaths were caused by Branch Davidians within the compound. The fire was ignited and spread by the Branch Davidians. They had murdered their own people, including the children. Our conclusions were beyond the shadow of a doubt. We had proved the negative. The theory, concocted by a documentary filmmaker and believed by 61 percent of the American people, had no basis in reality.

Since we found no grounds for the suspicions, one might ask why such an elaborate investigation was necessary. To some it might seem that we wasted a lot of time and money. But I don't think so. When 61 percent of the public believes that federal agents shoot at their fellow citizens, killing children, and intentionally set fire to a building filled with eighty or so souls, the relationship between the government and the people is destroyed.

The great founding principle of America, for which our Revolution was fought, is enshrined in the Declaration of Independence, that "government derives its just powers from the consent of the governed." That means that there must be a relationship between the people and their government. If government were not simply mistaken but evil, there would be no relationship. If that were the way America is, then the purpose of the Revolution would be lost. But it is not the way America is. Because conspiracy theories are destructive of the bond that connects us to each other and to our government, it's our responsibility as citizens to greet them with disbelief, and debunk them as we did with Waco.

Yet another way of avoiding responsibility for others is doing so in the name of grand philosophical principle. Such is the approach of libertarians who champion the philosophy of self-interest, a concept antithetical to religion. Since politicians who claim this philosophy are on the right of the ideological spectrum, they may be using the term "libertarian" as a shorthand way to appeal to their base by saying simply that they are more than normally conservative, they are extremely conservative. But conservatives and libertarians are not simply different in degree, they are different in kind. Conservatives espouse limited government. Libertarians believe that their greatest good, individualism, shouldn't be encumbered by responsibility to God or neighbor. The complaint against libertarianism does not concern specific items that may be in a political platform. Policy issues are always debatable by well-intentioned people. The complaint is against an underlying philosophy of selfishness that faithful people must oppose.

The libertarian banner is carried by an organization known as the Atlas Society, named after Ayn Rand's book *Atlas Shrugged* and dedicated to championing Rand's ideology. Several Republican politicians have used the Atlas Society as a forum for expressing their ideas, including Congressman Paul Ryan, who in 2005 told the society, "I grew up reading Ayn Rand and it taught me quite a bit about who I am and what my value systems are and what my beliefs are." My guess is that Congressman Ryan's comment was an exaggeration, designed to compliment his audience. Politicians tend to do this in their public appearances, beginning their speeches with comments like "No one has done more for the cause of liberty than Joe Doaks, who just introduced me," or "That was the best apple pie I ever tasted." So I would not hold Congressman Ryan to the generous comments he made to the Atlas Society. To the contrary, I think that libertarianism is inconsistent with the Christianity he practices and with the conservatism he ably represents. But the congressman was quite right in his use of the term "value systems." The libertarianism of Ayn Rand is a value system, not a bundle of policy positions on which conservatives may agree. So my criticism is not of specific stands on the size and cost of government, nor of politicians who take those stands. My criticism is of an underlying philosophy of egoism that is antithetical to America's religious and political traditions.

The libertarian philosophy can be summarized by quoting Ayn Rand's words:

- "I swear, by my life and my love of it, that I will never live for the sake of another man, nor ask another man to live for mine."*

* Ayn Rand, *Atlas Shrugged* (New York: Random House, 1957), part 3, chapter 1.

- "If any civilization is to survive, it is the morality of altruism that men have to reject."[*]
- "To say 'I love you' one must first be able to say the 'I.' "[†]
- "But why should you care what people will say? All you have to do is please yourself."[‡]

The implications of this philosophy for public policy are borne out by the platform of the Libertarian Party, which calls for the elimination of foreign aid as well as the elimination of "the entire social welfare system," including food stamps, subsidized housing, "and all the rest."

Libertarian egoism has nothing in common with the conservatism of Ronald Reagan and George W. Bush. In 1985, at a time of sub-Saharan drought and fighting, I made a two-week tour of the miserable condition of Africa, traveling to out-of-the-way settlements in places like Senegal and Mozambique where people were starving to the point of eating the bark off of trees. In no place that I visited did the United States have even the slightest degree of national self-interest. On the same afternoon that we returned to Washington, I went to the Oval Office to present the president with a hastily arranged slide show

[*] Ayn Rand, "Faith and Force: The Destroyers of the Modern World," lecture delivered at Yale University, New Haven, CT, February 17, 1960, fn.

[†] Ayn Rand, *The Fountainhead* (Indianapolis: Bobbs-Merrill, 1943), part 2, chapter 14.

[‡] Ibid.

featuring dust-swept huts and mothers holding dying children. As a result of President Reagan's leadership, the United States committed $50 million in emergency food aid to Africa. That would not have happened if President Reagan had followed the principle of selfishness advocated by Ayn Rand.

I had a similar experience under George W. Bush, who appointed me his special envoy for peace in Sudan. I am certain that the peace agreement between the Sudanese government and the rebels in the south would not have been reached without the personal engagement of President Bush. Here again, the national interest of the United States was at best remote. The same could be said for the forty-third president's effort to combat HIV/AIDS in Africa. That had nothing to do with the real politics of national interest, but it had everything to do with humanity.

In the 2016 presidential campaign, it would be interesting to ask the candidates if they agree with the philosophy of libertarian individualism in the Ayn Rand quotes set out above. Would a candidate say that if elected he or she "will never live for the sake of another man," or agree that, if elected, "All you have to do is please yourself." If that is the standard, then there is no such thing as public service, since the officeholder's sole interest would be serving the self.

Thankfully, there are people in public life who do not

follow the libertarian philosophy that the guiding principle of life is self-interest. The first example that comes to my mind is my lifelong friend Alex Netchvolodoff, who at age thirty-two left a promising career in retail to serve with low pay as my administrative assistant, first in the Missouri Attorney General's office, then in the U.S. Senate. He gave me more than two decades in what was the prime of his working life, winning great respect in Missouri and Washington, but with little of tangible value for himself. I once inscribed a photograph taken of the two of us with a citation from the Bible, "John 15:13." That verse reads, "No one has greater love than this, to lay down one's life for one's friends." We are blessed by knowing people like Alex Netchvolodoff whose lives are lived for others. They volunteer in soup kitchens or as mentors in inner-city schools. My dentist, Dennis Stovall, an ordained deacon in the Catholic Church, makes regular trips to South America to attend to people in impoverished villages. This is living the life of a faithful purpose, living beyond the self and following the example of a Lord who gave himself up to death and who called on us to take up our own crosses and follow him.

No serious American politician would go so far as some libertarian philosophers in directly attacking religion. In a book coauthored with Ayn Rand bearing the arresting title *The Virtue of Selfishness: A New Concept of Egoism,* Nathaniel Branden has said, "There is no greater self-delusion than to imagine that one can render unto reason that which is reason's and unto faith that which is faith's." Branden embellished his parody of the words of Jesus by saying, "Faith is a malignancy that no system can tolerate with impunity; and the man who succumbs to it, will call on it in precisely those issues where he needs his reason most."*

Few if any practical politicians hold the extreme anti-religious opinions of Nathaniel Branden, and if they do, they wouldn't express them, but the meaning of their philosophy is just the same. The libertarian enshrinement of the autonomous self is wholly incompatible with the religious commandment to love our neighbor.

The biblical account of the temptation of Jesus in the wilderness serves as the religious rebuttal to the libertarian philosophy. In the third temptation, "The devil took [Jesus] to a very high mountain and showed him all the kingdoms of the world and their splendor; and he said to him, 'All these I will give you if you fall down and worship me.' Jesus said to him, 'Away with you, Satan! For it is written, "Worship the Lord your God, and serve only him."'" As I interpret this passage, the devil is not an independent being with a red costume and a pitchfork. The devil is within us and the passage is about priorities.

* Nathaniel Branden, "Mental Health Versus Mysticism and Self-Sacrifice," in Ayn Rand and Nathaniel Branden, *The Virtue of Selfishness: A New Concept of Egoism* (New York: Signet, 1964), 34.

If we worship ourselves and focus single-mindedly on what serves our own interests, we may win for ourselves great success. We may gain all the kingdoms of the world. But the story of the third temptation teaches us that such self-exaltation is devil worship.

Conservatives agree on principles that should not include the single-minded selfishness of libertarianism. All conservatives believe that the welfare of America depends on a strong private sector including families, communities, and businesses. All conservatives oppose the burdens of excessive government. All conservatives believe in the benefits of free markets not overly weighed down by taxation and regulation. If all conservatives agree on these fundamentals, it is interesting to speculate on what some politicians think they gain by identifying themselves as libertarians. Probably they do this because they think that an appeal to selfishness has political advantage. Perhaps assurance that individual interests are for the greater good of America is just what voters want to hear, especially when that message is coupled with a claim that others, the government or the have-nots, are trying to take from them what they have worked so hard to make and keep. It is comforting, even inspiring, to learn that the welfare of the country and the future of the economy depend on better serving your own interests. But many people who hear such a message will detect in it a callousness toward others. Liberals certainly portray it that way, characterizing the philosophy of their opponents as being, "You're on your own." Many Americans agree with conservatives that the strength of the country is in the private sector and that excessive government is a dead weight that stunts our development. Many Americans would support conservatism provided that they don't detect within it any hint of meanness. The Republican Party as it is presented by its libertarian element comes across as being mean, especially in the eyes of women, minorities, and gays. An appearance of meanness may energize people for whom meanness is an attractive message. It may help win the support of voters in primary elections. But for the rest of the country it isn't a winning approach.

That libertarianism will never be widely acceptable by the American people is a tactical reason why conservatives should reject it. But the more significant reason has nothing to do with the practicalities of electoral politics. We should reject the philosophy of egoism because it is worse than bad politics; it is morally wrong. It is in opposition to the most basic principle of religion, the Love Commandment. It sets itself against the standard of the Cross. Libertarianism is in flat contradiction to what religion demands, and faithful people should say so.

The need to be admired is a leading motivator for many of us, especially those who are in politics. Now and then we hear about people who are on the take, but nearly all politicians I have known were honest and were not in it for the money. Most of my political acquaintances could have made more in the private sector where many would have found better job security. So, if not for money, why would anyone go into politics? For me and for many I knew, politics was interesting, challenging, often fun, and, hopefully, an opportunity to do some good. That was several decades ago. In the present dysfunctional state of affairs, one wonders whether any of that applies.

I think what motivates nearly all of us who have been in politics is the need to be admired by colleagues and constituents. For those in or aspiring to elective office, election day provides an accurate measure of admiration, at least relative to one's opponent. Of course, when politicians rank at the lowest level of public esteem, that may not mean much.

Through advertising and image making, politicians go to great expense to convince voters of their admirability. To a lesser extent, all of us do the same thing. Socially and in business, we present ourselves as attractively as we can.

The great historical champion of economic conservatism wasn't Ayn Rand, but Adam Smith, the eighteenth-century British philosopher. Smith was an advocate of free markets who believed that the hidden hand of competition rather than governmental control was the most efficient regulator of the marketplace. So lasting was his influence that during the Reagan administration, conservative economists wore neckties bearing the likeness of their hero. Smith's great work on economics was *The Wealth of Nations,* but his great contribution to our thinking about values was *The Theory of Moral Sentiments,* published in 1759.

Writing of the human tendency toward altruism, Smith asked what "prompts the generous upon all occasions, and the mean upon many, to sacrifice their own interests to the great interests of others?" He answered:

It is reason, principle, conscience, the inhabitant of the breast, the man within, the great judge and arbiter of our conduct. It is he who, whenever we are about to act so as to affect the happiness of others, calls to us, with a voice capable of astonishing the most presumptuous of our passions, that we are but one of the multitude, in no respect better than any other in it; and that when we prefer ourselves so shamefully and so blindly to others, we become the proper objects of resentment, abhorrence, and execration.[*]

He went on to say:

---

[*] Adam Smith, *The Theory of Moral Sentiments,* part III: "Of the Foundation of our Judgments concerning our own Sentiments and Conduct, and of the Sense of Duty," chapter 3.

When . . . violence and artifice prevail over sincerity and justice, what indignation does it not excite in the breast of every human spectator? What sorrow and compassion for the sufferings of the innocent, and what furious resentment against the success of the oppressor?[*]

Smith believed that altruism was prompted both by the voice of conscience, "the man within," and by the hope that one's praiseworthy actions would win the praise of others. This is the opposite of Ayn Rand's idea that "all you have to do is please yourself." He said:

What reward is most proper for promoting the practice of truth, justice, and humanity? The confidence, the esteem, and the love of those we live with. Humanity does not desire to be great but to be beloved. It is not in being rich that truth and justice would rejoice, but in being trusted and believed, recompenses which those virtues must almost always acquire.[†]

Smith's ambition to earn and receive praise was echoed by Abraham Lincoln in his first campaign address in 1832: "Every man is said to have his peculiar am-

[*] Ibid., chapter 5.
[†] Ibid.

bition. . . . I have no other so great as that of being truly esteemed by my fellow men, by rendering myself worthy of their esteem."

Ideally, all of us have a conscience that governs our behavior regardless of the consequences to ourselves. But in reality, most of us are attuned to the opinions of those who are around us. We want their esteem, and we want to avoid their abhorrence. This tendency to play to an audience that approves or disapproves of our conduct can impel us to self-sacrifice as suggested by Adam Smith. But the same desire to be what others expect us to be led German police officers to murder thirty-eight thousand Jews. What people think is not merely internal to them. It can have consequences for us, for good or for evil.

This is why the libertarian philosophy, espoused by Ayn Rand and approved by her admirers, is worse than a peculiar but merely theoretical ideology. It is an alternative value system that would create competing expectations for conduct that are incompatible with religion, and, as we shall see, it is incompatible with the founding principles of America. If politicians were being other than polite in their appearances before the Atlas Society, and if they meant to embrace Ayn Rand's value system, I hope they will rethink their opinions. Libertarianism is not conservatism. It is contrary to the most basic tenets of religion. It warrants our condemnation, not our praise.

. . .

The philosophy common to our founders was the opposite of libertarianism. They called it "virtue." We can think of virtue in two ways. In one use it means rectitude, conducting one's private life in the most upright way. In the other use, it means living beyond one's personal interests for the benefit of a higher calling. It's possible to be virtuous in one sense but not in the other. One politician may be straitlaced to the point of being puritanical in his deportment, but lacking in any generosity beyond himself. Another may be a brilliant public servant, but an incorrigible womanizer in his personal life. What is so for politicians is equally so for the public. We can imagine both the moralistic miser and the reprobate philanthropist.

Primarily, America's early presidents thought of virtue as the commitment to the public good over private interests. It was in sharp contrast to the libertarian concept of exalting individualism to the highest rank of our value system. Instead, our founders focused on containing self-interest both by the dispersal of political power and by the loyalty of our people to our common purpose. In their thinking, the future of America would depend at least as much on the virtue of our citizens as on the design of our government.

James Madison was the principal architect of our constitutional structure and, with Alexander Hamilton and

John Jay, one of the great advocates for its adoption. In *The Federalist Papers,* Nos. 10 and 51, the focus of his attention was what he called "factions" and we would call interest groups, combinations of citizens who band together to further their own purposes. Madison was a realist in his understanding of human nature. To be human is to try to advance one's own cause. The threat to liberty would occur when a faction grew so powerful that it could serve its own interests at the expense of the rights of others, a possibility that would become reality if an unbridled faction became a majority, the "tyranny of the majority." To prevent this from happening, Madison wanted to balance the interests of factions and to disperse the powers of government among its several branches. In his words, "Ambition must be made to counteract Ambition. The interest of the man must be connected with the constitutional rights of the place."* Contrary to libertarianism, his goal was not to get government out of the way so that self-interests would prevail, but to arrange government in such a way that the furtherance of self-interest would not be oppressive.

In *The Federalist,* No. 51, Madison summed up his realistic view of human nature and the attendant necessity of a well-ordered government:

---

* James Madison, *The Federalist,* No. 51.

It may be a reflection on human nature, that such devices should be necessary to control the abuses of government. But what is government itself, but the greatest of all reflections on human nature? If men were angels, no government would be necessary. If angels were to govern men, neither external nor internal controls on government would be necessary.

While he was realistic about our natural pursuit of our own causes and the need for a system of government to control us lest we become oppressive, Madison believed it essential that citizens bring more to our common enterprise than naked self-interest. Ultimately, no government, however well structured, would be sufficient without citizens who were dedicated to the common good. He described this dedication as a "great republican principle" and called it "virtue." At the Virginia Convention, convened to ratify the Constitution, Madison answered the objection that perhaps the people would elect a mischievous Congress:

I go on this great republican principle, that people will have virtue and intelligence to select men of virtue and wisdom. Is there no virtue among us? If there be not, we are in a wretched situation. No theoretical checks—no form of government can render us secure. To suppose that any form of government will secure liberty or happiness without any virtue in the people, is a chimerical idea.[*]

In his Farewell Address, George Washington expressed opinions similar to Madison's. Washington's concern was that a spirit of party would supplant our commitment to the good of the nation. Like Madison, he believed that this party spirit derived from human nature, and that a political system of checks and balances was necessary to contain it. And also like Madison, he believed that a virtuous citizenry would be essential to America's future: "It is substantially true that virtue or morality is a necessary spring of popular government," and "Of all the dispositions and habits which lead to political prosperity, religion and morality are indispensable supports."

Virtue was a theme of the early years of our republic. John Adams wrote that "liberty can no more exist without virtue and independence than the body can live and move without a soul."[†] He equated virtue with "passion for the public good," which he said "must be superior to all private passions":

---

[*] James Madison, *The Founders' Constitution* (Chicago: University of Chicago Press), volume 1, chapter 13, document 36.
[†] John Adams, *Novanglus and Massachusettensis: Political Essays* (1774, 1775), 25.

Public virtue cannot exist in a nation without private, and public virtue is the only foundation of republics. There must be a positive passion for the public good, the public interest, honor, power and glory, established in the minds of the people, or there can be no republican government, nor any real liberty: and this public passion must be superior to all private passions.*

In a handwritten reference, Thomas Jefferson quoted Montesquieu with approval: "Virtue may be defined as the love of the laws of our country. As such love requires a constant preference of public to private interest, it is the source of all private virtue."†

In sum, it is clear that in the minds of our first four presidents, the future of America would depend on more than the structure of our government; it would depend on the responsibility of the American people not only for their individual well-being but for the good of the whole.

An alternative to the founders' understanding of the primacy of the common good is the view that the best way to serve ourselves is to serve others, expecting something in

---

* John Adams, letter to Mercy Otis Warren, April 16, 1776.
† Charles, Second Baron of Brede and Montesquieu, *Spirit of the Laws* (1748), IV, chapter 5.

return, an approach to politics exemplified by the great and wily senator from Louisiana, Russell Long.

In January 1977, I had just started out in the Senate, a forty-year-old greenhorn, one of a powerless thirty-eight-member Republican minority and the most insignificant member of the Senate Finance Committee. The committee had jurisdiction over federal taxation, and it was chaired by Russell, whom I had never met before I showed up for my first day. As I arrived and took my place at the far end of the conference table, the committee was at work writing a letter to the Budget Committee that would set out the legislative plan for the year ahead. During a brief lull in the proceedings, I raised my hand and sought the chair's recognition.

"Mr. Chairman," I said, "I have an idea."

"Oh," said Russell Long, peering down the length of the table at the junior senator he had never met. "What's the Senator's idea?"

"I think we should have a tax cut," said I, voicing standard Republican philosophy.

"Oh, how much of a tax cut?" asked the chairman.

Well, I had never thought about that, so I blurted out the first number that popped into my head: "$5 billion." In those days, $5 billion was real money.

"Is there any objection?" Russell asked the committee. Hearing none, he added, "All right, that's agreed to."

My first thought was, "Wow! Life in the Senate is going to be great!" Quickly, I rushed back to my office and cranked out a press release telling Missourians that on my first day on the job I had reduced taxes by $5 billion. It was a political bonanza.

Of course, I had done no such thing. The Finance Committee was writing a letter, not passing a law. Russell Long wasn't legislating, he was making me look good to my constituents, doing me a favor even though I was the newest and most lowly member of his committee. I wondered why he did this favor for me.

The answer became clear eight years later after Republicans had taken control of the Senate and I had become chairman of the Commerce Committee. Tape recorder in hand, I visited Russell in his office to ask his thoughts on how to be an effective chairman. He offered two pieces of advice. One was never to hold a grudge against another senator, because my opponent in today's battle could be my ally tomorrow. The other was to give every member of the committee a stake in the legislation I was trying to pass. This was easily accomplished in tax bills, Russell's special expertise. They were mammoth, with many sections, so it was a simple matter to add something for another senator. Each committee member had constituent interests to accommodate or a point of view to advance. Russell's idea was that if he satisfied each senator on some particular matter, all members of the committee would support passage of the bill.

Russell's reasoning in agreeing to my proposed tax cut was similar to his approach to moving legislation. Even on my first day, he wanted to include me in the work of his committee. If I had a stake in the committee's success, I would be his partner when the real work of legislating commenced.

The expression "logrolling" has a sinister connotation of vote trading, that is, the agreement to support another member's cause in exchange for the reciprocal promise to support yours. But the great master of the Senate, Russell Long, was far subtler and, I think, more principled than that, and more consistent with how ordinary people act in everyday life. Russell's belief was that when we support other people, they will support us. We help ourselves by helping others. His approach created a cooperative atmosphere in the Finance Committee where members understood that they could best serve their own interests when they supported the interests of their colleagues. The spirit of mutual support depended neither on seniority nor on party. Russell Long was the senior Democrat on the committee. I was the junior Republican.

Nearly a century and a half before my first day on the Finance Committee, French philosopher and observer of

America Alexis de Tocqueville advanced a theory that would have appealed to Russell Long of why citizens would look beyond their immediate personal concerns for the sake of the common good. While Tocqueville left open the possibility that Americans might yield "to the disinterested, spontaneous impulses that are part of man's nature,"* he said little about the virtuous love of country that was emphasized by the founders. Instead, Tocqueville believed that people are motivated almost entirely by self-interest, but of a sort different from the self-absorbed individualism of libertarians. Self-interest, he thought, was best served not by isolating oneself from the world, but by joining forces with associations of like-minded people. He called this banding together with others to serve one's purposes "self-interest properly understood,"† and said, "As soon as common affairs are dealt with in common, each man sees that he is not as independent of his fellow men as he initially imagined and that, in order to obtain their support, he must often lend them his cooperation."‡

Tocqueville's criticism was directed at individualism, not self-interest. He defined individualism as withdrawing "into a circle of family and friends" and leaving the

* Alexis de Tocqueville, *Democracy in America* (New York: Library of America, 2004), 611.
† Ibid., part II, chapter 8.
‡ Ibid., 590.

larger society to take care of itself.* He thought that this disconnection from fellow citizens carried the seeds of despotism.† The connectedness and cooperation Tocqueville praised was rooted in private associations of citizens who shared the same interests, such as groups of farmers. He believed that associations of citizens rather than government were capable of advancing the "feelings and ideas of a great nation." For government to attempt such a mission would be for Tocqueville "an intolerable tyranny."‡

In sum, Tocqueville thought that the American commitment to the common good had little to do with virtue and much to do with "self-interest properly understood." I will help you, because that will help me. We will join together in associations so that we and other members can help each other.

In the twentieth century, Tocqueville's idea that mutual self-interest accounts for cooperation in seeking the common good was taken up by the field of mathematics known as game theory. A question mathematicians addressed was how to explain the persistence of altruism given Charles Darwin's theory that the fittest, strongest, and most aggressive of a species survived the evolutionary process. It would be reasonable to assume that in a

* Ibid., 585.
† Ibid., 590.
‡ Ibid., 598.

world of rough-and-tumble competition, the altruistic would fall by the wayside, but that has not been the case. The famous game that mathematicians developed to explore this quandary was called "the prisoner's dilemma." Two people suspected of a crime are isolated from each other and separately offered a deal. If one prisoner informs on the other and the first remains silent, the informer will go free and the accused will be sentenced to a term of ten years. If each informs on the other, each will receive a five-year sentence. If each remains silent, the sentence for each will be one year.

The best combined result for the two players would be for each to act altruistically and not inform on the other. But because they cannot communicate with each other, neither can be sure what the other will do. The solution for the game theorists was for the players to understand the actions of one another by observation in the absence of words. If the players were allowed to play the game over and over, they would eventually understand the actions of the other prisoner and act accordingly. This was called the iterated prisoner's dilemma, and the process of experiencing and simply imitating the other player's last move was called tit-for-tat.*

Tocqueville believed that we help other people be-

* For a clear explanation of game theory, to which I am indebted, see Jonathan Sacks, *The Dignity of Difference: How to Avoid the Clash of Civilizations* (London: Continuum, 2002), chapter 8.

cause it is in our best interests to do so. That is his "self-interest properly understood." The prisoner's dilemma adds that we gain an understanding of how to advance our self-interest by experiencing the actions of others, and we develop a method of responding—tit-for-tat. We do what we experience other people doing. According to the prisoner's dilemma, when we act for the benefit of others we are doing so in response to what we experience rather than in furtherance of an abstract principle of altruism. The same can be said of biblical religion where our expected conduct is the consequence of our experience, that of God working in history. Biblical ethics isn't an abstraction such as "Honesty is the best policy" or "Think globally and act locally." It is our appropriate reaction to God's action. The Bible is an account of revelation, God's interaction with the world, and instruction on how we should live in light of that revelation.

The Ten Commandments are more than a list of rules that appear without context. They are commandments to the people of Israel on how to live in relation to God who delivered Israel through events. They begin with a preamble that creates an historical setting: "I am the Lord your God, who brought you out of the land of Egypt, out of the house of slavery" (Exodus 20:2). Transgressions violate more than a code of conduct, they violate the relationship that the God of history has created with God's people:

Hear this word that the Lord has spoken against you O people of Israel, against the whole family that I brought up out of the land of Egypt: You only have I known of all the families of the earth; therefore I will punish you for all your iniquities. (Amos 3:1–2)

Again, in the New Testament, how we are expected to live is directly connected to our experience of God in history, God coming into the world in Jesus Christ. Thomas Jefferson attempted to detach the teachings of Jesus from theology, and was left with nice words and no substance. Christian ethics is more than attention to the teachings of Jesus, it is a response to our experience of the presence of God in Christ. As expressed in the First Letter of John, "We love because he first loved us" (1 John 4:19).

We learn how to live from what we experience. That is the teaching of the Bible. It is borne out by the prisoner's dilemma. The corollary is that people around us learn how to live from their experience of how we live.

The prisoner's dilemma demonstrated that for reciprocity to work, each party must know what the other is doing, if not through verbal communication then by experience. Tocqueville's concept of self-interest properly understood turns on our knowing that we have mutual interests with other people, and that in advancing their interests we serve our own. The notion of a common good has no meaning without commonality. But what if we are not aware of what others are doing? What if we remain in our isolated rooms as in the prisoner's dilemma and remain ignorant of the other player's actions? That is the phenomenon described in Robert Putnam's *Bowling Alone*. In the last few decades of the twentieth century, we began dropping out of groups that had bound us together and we started turning in on ourselves. We have exchanged social interaction in bowling leagues and PTAs for isolation in automobiles and in front of TV screens. As our time alone has grown, our civic responsibility has shrunk.

Putnam believes that the shift from "us" to "me" occurred in the last third of the twentieth century. I recall the afternoon it became obvious to me. It was in early 1982 during a phone call with my friend and political filmmaker Charles Guggenheim. I was running for reelection to the Senate, and thought that the unsustainability of Medicare and Social Security would be a burden on future generations. Social Security has long been considered the "third rail" of politics—touch it and you're dead. But it seemed to me that there would be enormous upside to making a straightforward appeal for the long-term future of America. I even had a catchy phrase in mind that I thought should be the slogan of the campaign: "What About Our Children?" Brimming with enthusiasm, I phoned Charles with my bright idea, but was brought to earth by his sound advice. "If you ask, 'What about our children?' voters will reply, 'What about us?' They won't be interested in the future, they will only care about now." In other words, forget about our children. It's all about ourselves.

Robert Putnam has made an impressive case that we have depleted our social capital by separating ourselves from our neighbors. Still, I believe that even in self-isolation, there's a longing for connection to the nation and to our communities. Crowds that chant, "USA, USA," at Olympic games thrill at being identified with our country. At times of disaster, citizens draw close to their communities. After terrorists exploded bombs near the finish line of the Boston Marathon, killing and horribly maiming spectators, residents of the city took pride in what they wanted to believe was their common trait, and wore T-shirts with the legend "Boston Strong." After a gunman entered Sandy Hook Elementary School in Newtown, Connecticut, and massacred children, the frequently heard statement of citizens was, "We're a tight-knit community." In fact, that has become the predictable response of communities at times of tragedy. I recall watching a TV interview of a Cleveland resident after the discovery that three young women had been imprisoned in a house for more than a decade. For years, people who lived next door and across the street had observed the comings and goings of the homeowner without any idea that the house was a prison. Remarkably, the person interviewed said, "We're a tight-knit neighborhood."

Whether these boasts are true is at best doubtful. Residents of Boston are probably no more strong or weak than people in any other city. They probably spend the same number of hours sitting silently before their television sets or behind the wheels of their cars or bowling alone. It is hard to believe that Clevelanders who are oblivious to a decade of imprisoned women on their street live in a "tight-knit neighborhood." But that's not the point. What is significant is that it is important for people to see themselves this way. They do not want the self-image of isolated souls who huddle behind walls with little connection to others. They want to be part of something bigger than themselves, so they don T-shirts announcing that they, like their neighbors, are Boston Strong, or they say that they are tightly knit into their community.

We do not want to be alone. We long to be connected. And if this is what people want, perhaps there are ways to help them get there.

Earlier, I told the story of being at a baseball game when a young man loudly and crudely offended everyone within earshot. To my regret, I did nothing to stop him. A different story was told in *The New York Times* by a woman who described her experience of moving to my hometown:

In fact, we got an early clue as to what kind of place St. Louis is during our first summer here, at a

Cardinals-Cubs game. Sitting behind us in the stadium was a guy who looked to be about 20 and drunk. As people walked by, he'd yell out mocking observations about their appearances. Finally, I turned and said, "You know, everyone else here just wants to enjoy the game like you do." . . . I half expected the guy to slug me. Instead, looking taken aback, he said, "I hadn't thought of it like that. I'm sorry." I was stunned into silence.*

I make two points about this story. First, no matter how purposefully the young man acted to alienate himself from other people, when addressed by another, he responded as one who wanted to be part of his surroundings. Second, the woman at the ball game took it upon herself to do something to make the situation better.

Where do we go to find more people who, like the new resident of St. Louis, will call us to our better nature? Let's examine two possibilities, politics and religion, and consider which offers the better prospect of inspiring us to look beyond ourselves to the common good.

In his inaugural address, John F. Kennedy famously said, "And so, my fellow Americans: ask not what your country can do for you—ask what you can do for your country."

---

* Curtis Sittenfeld, "Loving the Midwest," *New York Times,* June 8, 2013.

Earlier in that same short speech, the new president said, "Let every nation know, whether it wishes us well or ill, that we shall pay any price, bear any burden, meet any hardship, support any friend, oppose any foe, in order to assure the survival and the success of liberty."

It was an eloquent appeal to all Americans to subordinate their self-interest to the common good and make whatever sacrifices would be necessary for "the survival and the success of liberty," and it showed us, at least for a moment, that politicians can call on us for something more than service of self. But Kennedy's speech was made on January 20, 1961, and it stands alone. In the more than half a century since that speech it is hard—I think impossible—to recall any American politician saying anything in the same vein as Kennedy did, much less anything approaching the same inspirational force. Indeed, with very few exceptions—Lincoln's second inaugural is one—the political concept of virtue passed from the scene with the deaths of our first four presidents. Today's politics is not the balancing of competing interests leavened by virtue as envisioned by James Madison. It is the naked appeal to self-interest alone.

There is nothing elevating, nothing Kennedyesque about today's politics. Many people lament the nasty tone of election campaigns that consist of relentless personal attacks delivered in twenty-second bursts, but TV commercials are not the only or even the most serious defect in our politics. The real problem is that campaigns begin and end with appeals to the self-interest of voters. It's as though the message of both parties and all candidates is, "I'm for you and against them."

Far away from announcing confidently that Americans will "pay any price, bear any burden, and meet any hardship," no politician asks likely supporters to pay any price at all, bear even the lightest burden, or tolerate the slightest hardship, even if it is clear, as it is with a nearly $20 trillion national debt, that the survival and success of liberty is at stake. The standard political message is that the recipients of government largesse are only getting what they rightly deserve. Indeed, the large transfer payment programs led by Social Security and Medicare are appropriately called "entitlement programs." We participate in them because we are entitled to do so, even though what we paid in is only a fraction of what we will receive.

The code word of modern politics is "fairness." What voters hear is not that their self-interests will be promoted if they elect one candidate over another, but that, at long last, they will be treated fairly. Here's the gist of the message: "You, the American people, are treated unfairly. You are asked to do too much. The burden is too heavy on you. The other side doesn't listen to you. If it did listen to you, it would not treat you so unfairly. Do you know what is unfair? Your taxes are too high. Your benefits are too low." That's the basic message politicians give to the American people, because it is more appealing to say that we Americans should feel sorry for ourselves than to say that we should grab as much for ourselves as we can.

In addition to claiming unfairness, another way to disguise self-interest is to dress it up in the guise of altruism. Many Americans across the political spectrum would agree that government has a special duty to help the poor. But much of what the federal government does is help the nonpoor. It's common to blame the government's budget problems on waste and inefficiency, but about two-thirds of what the federal government spends is in check-writing programs directly to (e.g., Social Security) or on behalf of (e.g., Medicare) individuals, with little waste or inefficiency. Three-fourths of what government spends on such transfer programs is not based on need. For example, I am a beneficiary of Social Security and Medicare, although I am not needy. Putting it another way, about half of what the federal government spends (three-quarters of two-thirds) is on check-writing programs that are not related to need.

Let's look at the tax side of the federal budget. Tax expenditures such as deductions and credits that reduce a person's tax bill are economically equivalent to payments received from the government. That is, reducing the amount of a check one sends the government is the same as receiving a check from the government. In 2013, the top ten federal tax expenditures* were worth $926 billion, or 5.7 percent of gross domestic product (GDP). Seventeen percent of these tax expenditures were for the top 1 percent of the income scale, and 8 percent of the benefit was for the bottom 20 percent. In other words, the dollar value of tax expenditures for the top 1 percent is more than double the value for the bottom 20 percent.

I do not make this point to suggest a wholesale dumping of tax expenditures or an increased level of taxation on the American people. My personal view is that the federal government's share of GDP should be at its historic rate of about 20 percent or lower, and that tax reform consisting of reduced rates and less generous expenditures would be desirable. My point here is simply that government spending in the form of transfer payments and its equivalent in tax expenditures is efficient, and that the leading beneficiaries are the nonpoor.

We are neither pitiful souls who are denied our just deserts from government nor altruists giving of ourselves in aid of the less fortunate. While we like to hear that more for us is only fair and that our aim is to help the

---

* Exclusions from taxable income for employer-sponsored health insurance, net pension contributions and earnings, capital gains on assets transferred at death, and a portion of Social Security and Railroad Retirement benefits; itemized deductions for certain taxes paid to state and local governments, mortgage interest payments, and charitable contributions; preferential tax rates on capital gains and dividends; and tax credits for earned income and child care.

poor, we have designed a government to serve our economic self-interest. We reward politicians who build on that concept and keep it intact. We penalize politicians who threaten our self-interest. Should we expect politics to call us to look beyond ourselves to the common good? The lesson of history is that we should not.

Now let's consider religion as a source of virtue. I lived in New York City in the mid-1960s, practicing law during the week and my ministry on Sundays, when I began the day taking Communion to bedsides in New York Hospital. Many who asked for the sacrament were in extreme conditions. In that era, radical amputation was a standard way of treating cancer. I recall a patient who had just had both legs amputated at the hips. Others knew that death was near. For a newly ordained priest, it taught a lot about the grace with which people of faith face disaster or the end of life. A lawyer named Charles Buckley made a special impression on me. He had been hospitalized after the most recent of several serious heart attacks, and understood that he did not have long to live. During one of my visits, after clearly expressing his strong belief in God's love, he told me that he didn't think the number of days he had left was of utmost importance. I took this not as an expression of resignation but as a statement of faith. Far from "hanging on for dear life," he saw himself in relation to God.

I have witnessed that same serenity in others on the verge of death, including my brother Don's peaceful joy on the night he succumbed to ALS. In these faithful people there is no desperate plea to be spared or complaint that suffering could come to them. Indeed, it is as though their plight is not the center of their attention. The mark of their faith is that their focus is not on themselves.

Of course, it's only human for us to focus on ourselves, especially when we are in extremis, and to see religion not as God-centered but as us-centered. Please, God, help me! We promise to live good lives so that God will favor us. Let's make a deal. Alexis de Tocqueville saw religion in connection with his concept of "self-interest properly understood." He thought that religion was capable of evoking goodness and altruism in believers by offering them something in return, happiness in the next world.* No doubt personal benefit, immediate or eternal, is a strong motivation for some religious people. If we think we have a quid pro quo relationship with God, it's in our best interest to be on our best behavior. But our relationship with God is not quid pro quo. To the contrary, it's as described in the Gospel's story of the rich young man (Matthew 19:16–26).

In the story, a rich young man asks Jesus, "What good deed must I do to have eternal life?" Jesus responds with

* Alexis de Tocqueville, *Democracy in America,* volume 2, part II, chapter 9.

the kind of automatic answer he must have given any number of times. If the questioner wants eternal life, he should obey the commandments: Don't murder, commit adultery, steal, or bear false witness; honor your parents, and love your neighbor as yourself. When the young man asks for a fuller answer, Jesus tells him to sell his possessions and give the proceeds to the poor. The young man departs in distress, and Jesus tells his disciples, "It is easier for a camel to go through the eye of a needle than for someone who is rich to enter the kingdom of God." He then adds, "For mortals it is impossible, but for God all things are possible."

The hope that God will open his kingdom to us despite our shortcomings is the Easter message. By the redeeming work of Christ, God overcomes the sin of the world and accepts us as we are. In the end, we are justified by faith and not by our works, which, as Paul emphasized, always fall short of the mark. But the story of the rich young man tells us that God's grace does not render our actions irrelevant. Jesus never suggests that because salvation is in God's hands the young man should do whatever he likes. To the contrary, the young man has walked away "grieving" when Jesus speaks hopeful words to the disciples. The young man never hears any hint that he is free to live any sort of life he pleases because all will be forgiven him by a gracious God. Instead, he gets the message that if he is to inherit the kingdom, a great deal of responsibility is on his shoulders.

The first thing he learns is moralistic, that his personal conduct is critically important. To inherit the kingdom he must obey the commandments. He must refrain from bad acts, murder, stealing, and adultery, and he must love his neighbor as himself. Jesus doesn't gloss over morality. It is at the top of the list when he speaks about the kingdom. People who seek the kingdom have the personal responsibility of living upright lives.

Next, the young man learns that if he wishes to be perfect he should sell his possessions and give the proceeds to the poor. This is a standard of perfection that monastics follow, and few others, but it contains a message of broad application: In pursuit of the kingdom, serving self-interest must not be of primary importance. He who loses his life will find it. Our model for the Christian life isn't the ambitious self-seeker who grabs as much for himself as he can, but the servant Messiah who empties himself of equality with God and takes the form of a slave (Philippians 2:6–7). The whole approach of the rich young man was upside down. He had everything earthly riches could provide him, so next on his list was winning for himself a place in the kingdom of God. What must I do to secure for myself my eternal life? For the rich young man, religion like everything else existed to serve his self-interest.

The rich young man equated the kingdom of God with eternal life. It was a future state to be accomplished by a victorious Messiah at the end of time. This was the understanding of the church from the time of the apostles who believed that Christ's return in glory was imminent, and that it would bring about a general resurrection of the dead. Today, when we say the Lord's Prayer, we pray that the kingdom, not now present, will come, but I doubt that many of us are asking God to bring about the immediate end of the world. The story of the raising of Lazarus teaches that the kingdom we expect to come in the future is already with us (John 11:17ff.). After Jesus tells Martha, "Your brother will rise again," she responds with the Pharisaic, future-oriented understanding of the resurrection, "I know that he will rise again in the resurrection on the last day." Jesus then responds in the present tense, "I am the resurrection and the life." In Jesus, the kingdom of God is both yet to come—that is, not fully realized—and already present.

Moreover, we are more than passive observers of God's work in establishing the kingdom. We are active participants. So we ask for strength, "our daily bread," to do our work in expanding the kingdom. This is what is known as the covenantal relationship between God and the people of God. God promises to be our God, active in our world, and we promise to be God's people, working to further the kingdom of God on earth.

A description of the kingdom of God, inaugurated by Christ and to be advanced by us, is set forth in the eleventh chapter of Isaiah:

> A shoot shall come out from the stump of Jesse, and a branch shall grow out of his roots. The spirit of the Lord shall rest on him, the spirit of wisdom and understanding, the spirit of counsel and might, the spirit of knowledge and the fear of the Lord. His delight shall be in the fear of the Lord. He shall not judge by what his eyes see, or decide by what his ears hear; but with righteousness he shall judge the poor, and decide with equity for the meek of the earth; he shall strike the earth with the rod of his mouth, and with the breath of his lips he shall kill the wicked. Righteousness shall be the belt around his waist, and faithfulness the belt around his loins. The wolf shall live with the lamb, the leopard shall lie down with the kid, the calf and the lion, and the fatling together, and a little child shall lead them. The cow and the bear shall graze, their young shall lie down together; and the lion shall eat straw like the ox. The nursing child shall play over the hole of the asp, and the weaned child shall put its hand on the adder's den. They will not hurt or destroy on all my holy mountain; for the earth will be full of the knowledge of the Lord as the waters cover the sea.

Isaiah's vision of the kingdom differs from the solid-gold, jewel-encrusted New Jerusalem described in detail in Revelation 21. It is about qualities rather than architecture, qualities we should seek to advance when we do the work of expanding God's kingdom. The qualities enumerated by Isaiah are righteousness for the poor, equity for the meek, and the pursuit of peace.

Matthew 25 paints a vivid picture of the Last Judgment in which the Son of Man sits on a throne and separates the sheep from the goats. Those who are welcomed into the kingdom have given food to the hungry, drink to the thirsty, welcome to the stranger, clothing to the naked, care to the sick, and companionship to prisoners. The goats who are consigned to eternal fire are the ones who have ignored the needs of "the least of these." Our obligation to care for the disadvantaged is a consistent theme in the Bible.* A standard grace said before meals in our family and at many dinner tables reflects this obligation. It asks God to "make us always mindful of the needs of others."

Understandably, our obligation to help the poor leads many people to see government as the most practical and efficient way to accomplish this. Government is where the money is. Government has the experience and the means to put resources in the right hands. After I saw the

---

* See, e.g., Proverbs 14:31, Psalm 41, Amos 5:11.

desperate plight of starving people in Africa, my first stop was the White House. My next stops were the relevant congressional committees. It would have been impossible to avert catastrophe without prompt and massive help from Washington. In their enthusiasm for limited government, some conservatives have demonstrated a "let them eat cake" attitude to those in need, and have seemed mean, sometimes outrageously so, in the process. Consider this report of an exchange between Wolf Blitzer and Congressman Ron Paul during a 2012 debate of Republican presidential hopefuls sponsored by the Tea Party Express:

> CNN moderator Wolf Blitzer's hypothetical question about whether an uninsured 30-year-old working man in [a] coma should be treated prompted one of the most boisterous moments of audience participation in the CNN/Tea Party Express [debate].
>
> "What he should do is whatever he wants to do and assume responsibility for himself," Paul responded, adding, "That's what freedom is all about, taking your own risk. This whole idea that you have to compare and take care of everybody . . ."
>
> The audience erupted into cheers, cutting off the Congressman's sentence.
>
> After a pause, Blitzer followed up by asking "Congressman, are you saying that society should

just let him die?" to which a small number of audience members shouted "Yeah!"[*]

As some conservatives have been mean-spirited in their rush to distance government from the needs of the poor and sick, some liberals have conflated their obligation to the poor and certainty about their favored policy positions. During consideration of Medicaid expansion by the Missouri General Assembly, an Episcopal priest in St. Louis sent an extensive memorandum to the clergy citing Matthew 25 and stating that "the faith we profess and the community to which we are bound as the Body of Christ, the church, demand our advocacy on behalf of the most vulnerable among us." That statement is, I think, beyond dispute. However, the specific advocacy urged by the memorandum is on behalf of Medicaid expansion, and that, as a means of helping "the least of these," *is* in dispute. A study published in the May 2013 edition of *The New England Journal of Medicine* reported that Medicaid expansion in Oregon led to increased utilization of health care services with "no significant improvement in measured physical health outcomes."[†]

[*] Amy Bingham, "Tea Party Debate Audience Cheered Idea of Letting Uninsured Patients Die," ABC News, September 13, 2011, http://abcnews go.com/blogs/politics/2011/09/tea-party-debate-audience-cheered-idea -of-letting-uninsured-patients-die/.

[†] Katherine Baicker, Ph.D., et al., "The Oregon Experiment—Effects of Medicaid on Clinical Outcomes," *New England Journal of Medicine*

If correct, the study published in *The New England Journal of Medicine* suggests that Medicaid expansion increases the utilization of physicians and hospitals, but that there may be more effective ways of helping the needy, such as improving schools or growing the economy. Perhaps further analysis would support the thesis of the clergy memorandum and show that Medicaid expansion is indeed the best bet for helping the poor.

In his recent book *Why Government Fails So Often: And How It Can Do Better,* Peter Schuck argues that many expensive government programs that were intended to help the poor in fact serve the well-off. He reports that from 1995 to 2012, farm subsidies cost $256 billion, with 90 percent of price support programs going to the top 20 percent of farms, while "the vast majority" received nothing.[*] Similarly, says Schuck, student aid transfers resources from the less to the more well-off, with relatively few subsidies going to low-income families. Schuck concludes, "This skewing of benefits to the middle and upper class is unsurprising; politicians across the political spectrum use the program in their appeals to better-off voters."[†] My point is simply that while our religious obli-

---

368 (May 2, 2013): 1713–22, http://www.nejm.org/doi/full/10.1056/NEJMsa1212321.

[*] Peter H. Schuck, *Why Government Fails So Often and How It Can Do Better* (Princeton, NJ: Princeton University Press, 2014), 242.

[†] Ibid., 260, 281.

gation to be mindful of the needy is beyond debate, how we translate that obligation into policy is debatable, as are almost all political questions. Politics is only politics, it isn't religion, and to be certain that one's political position is absolutely the best of all alternatives is to confuse the two.

I have high regard for Jim Wallis and his commitment to serve the poor through advocacy, but I question his tendency to identify his political opinions with the will of God. After identifying what he claims are wrong choices in the federal budget, including "wasteful military spending," subsidies to "huge corporations," and insufficiently high taxes on "the wealthiest among us," he adds, "And from a Christian point of view, it is also the wrong and immoral choice, completely conformed to the logic of the world employed by the most powerful and completely contrary to the biblical logic of the kingdom of God and Matthew 25."*

It has become fashionable for liberals to call the federal budget a "moral document," suggesting that one's budget priorities are moral and those of one's opponents are immoral. Such a dualistic view of politics shuts off debate and makes compromise, the essential component of writing budgets, difficult if not impossible. There is no

---

* Jim Wallis, *On God's Side: What Religion Forgets and Politics Hasn't Learned About Serving the Common Good* (Grand Rapids, MI: Brazos Press, 2013), 78.

humility in calling one's opponents "wrong and immoral" and "completely contrary to the biblical logic." It precludes valuable input of alternative opinions, even if we end up rejecting those alternatives.

When I visited a sprawling camp of starving refugees in Mozambique, experts told me that food aid to help those people would have the adverse consequences of depressing local food production and prolonging the stay of refugees in dense populations where it would never be possible for them to move beyond the most abject existence. The experts said that development assistance, not food aid, was the better way to help hungry people. My own view that I advocated to President Reagan was that food aid was the way to go, because without immediate relief the people would simply die. I was quite adamant in stating that position, but I never thought that the advocates of development assistance were immoral. They merely had a different opinion, and their opinion needed to be heard.

Because many faithful people think government is the most effective way to help the disadvantaged and advance the kingdom of God, there is a tendency to see one's religious responsibility discharged principally if not exclusively by attempting to influence government policy. During my Senate years, I called on a colleague of considerable wealth to solicit a charitable contribution to his college alma mater. I had no doubt that my fellow senator could easily make a six-figure gift to a college for which he professed high regard and that had a generous assistance program for underprivileged students. My colleague said he would make no more than a token contribution because in his role as a senator he had done his part by being instrumental in creating a government grant program for needy students. He felt excused from doing much personally because he had persuaded the government to do a lot fiscally. Similarly, some church-people have thought that their main work for the poor consisted in lobbying government. An Episcopal priest once told me that he had never attended a clergy conference that did not conclude with a resolution to write letters to Congress.

In 2012, the triennial General Convention of the Episcopal Church adopted forty-one resolutions urging action by government. Among other policies, the convention called on the president and Congress to:

- Admit the District of Columbia as a state;
- Enact stricter usury laws;
- Minimize military exercises near the DMZ in Korea;
- End the economic embargo against Cuba;
- Enact a carbon fuels tax or cap-and-trade regulations; and
- Adopt a "bold new program, solely focused on the creation of new jobs."

In addition, resolutions passed by the General Convention promised to:

- Study "issues surrounding the development of genetically engineered crop plants"; and
- Prepare "recommendations for military commanders on the use of drones."

Because it is unimaginable that in adopting such resolutions the General Convention was expressing the opinions of the entirety, or even a majority, of the Episcopal Church, and because the membership of the church comprises less than two-thirds of 1 percent of the population of the United States, the resolutions were of no consequence to politicians, even if they captured their attention. Because the General Convention has no known expertise on such matters as military exercises in Korea and genetically engineered plants, the resolutions will carry no weight with policymakers. But churches and churchpeople should not stop speaking just because their advice will not prevail. When Isaiah received his commission to speak for God, God told the prophet that his words would go unattended (Isaiah 6). If the church is convinced that it is expressing God's truth, its work is to bear witness to that truth, whether or not its witness affects public policy. While I personally doubt that God has spoken to the General Convention of the Episcopal

Church on, say, statehood for the District of Columbia, I would never suggest that officials who think they have heard God's voice should remain silent. I would, however, suggest humility in assuming that any political opinion held by the governing body of a church is shared by God.

But my main concern is not about what the General Convention did when it adopted forty-one resolutions urging government to act. My main concern is what the General Convention did not do. It spoke many words about the responsibilities of government, and, with only two exceptions, it said nothing about the responsibilities of people, including its own members. One of the exceptions was quite narrow. A resolution called for "steward leaders" to practice tithing. The other resolution, while it appealed to church members, was itself political. It called upon every member of the Episcopal Church to "make a moral commitment" to support Obamacare.

The 77th General Convention of the Episcopal Church issued forty-one appeals for governmental action, but was silent on what our first four presidents thought would be essential to America's success: virtue. It said not a word about how people conduct their lives, nothing about their responsibility to children and families, nothing about alcohol and drug use, and nothing about sexual promiscuity. It said nothing about subordinating self-interest to others, nothing about responsibility to one's community and the country, nothing about the common good. The answer the General Convention would have given the rich young man would have been quite different from the answer given by Jesus: Forget the commandments; enjoy self-service; write your member of Congress.

This is religion on the cheap, the bargain-basement cost of discipleship, and it's in perfect alignment with what now passes for ethics: the smug assurance that I should be free to do my own thing, especially with my own body, so long as I take correct positions on cap-and-trade legislation and GMO crops. What could be easier than to tell someone else, namely politicians, what they should be doing? Literally in this view, you don't have to lift a finger to be a perfectly good Christian. You can do it all with your thumbs. You can tweet your senator with instructions to tax this or spend on that, and then enjoy the rest of your day while religious leaders endorse your tweet and honor your choices of personal conduct.

Emphasis on political advocacy over comportment does more than create a cheap substitute for personal responsibility; it provides license for behavior that is abhorrent and destructive of the common good. Columnist Peggy Noonan made this point in commenting on the coarsening of discourse, especially in the outbreak of crude sexual slurs against women in public life. She noted that "leaders who are women are publicly demeaned and diminished just because they are women," and added:

> Here are some of the words that have been hurled the past few years at public figures who are female: "slut," "whore," "prostitute," "bimbo." You know the other, coarser words that have been used. But the point is, these are not private insults. They are said in public. This is something new in American political life, that women can be spoken of this way.[*]

Noonan reserved her harshest criticism for media personalities who claim that their "correct" positions on social issues, especially abortion, give them license to speak this way about women.

Political activism is important to our country, and it can be connected to our faith. Through it, we can improve the welfare of our people, especially those whom Matthew 25 calls "the least of these." But political activism is no substitute for the way we conduct our lives, and it must not serve as our excuse for avoiding the virtuous citizenship on which America depends.

I don't want to paint with too broad a brush and suggest that all religious people and all denominations are so absorbed by large political issues that they have lost

[*] Peggy Noonan, "America's Real War on Women," *Wall Street Journal*, March 16, 2012.

their focus on personal responsibility. Clearly, that is not the case. Some religions are quite demanding. I have in mind friends who are observant Jews whose faith governs every detail of their lives. Perhaps my comments relate mainly to mainline Protestantism and the Episcopal Church to which I belong. But I do believe that religion as I know it asks too little of its members, far less than America needs. Perhaps that is why the mainline churches are declining so markedly. It's as though their members have concluded that going to church isn't worth the effort.

Matthew D. Lieberman is a professor at UCLA and a pioneer in the new field of social cognitive neuroscience, who uses functional magnetic resonance imaging (fMRI) to study the brain as it responds to the pains and pleasures of social interactions. By focusing on different regions of the brain, fMRI gives us pictures of how we are "wired," that is, how we inherently react to various experiences in our interpersonal relations.

Lieberman reports that human beings are both self-interested and altruistic, and that our interest in the welfare of others is "part of our basic wiring."[*] He defines altruism as helping people when the long-term consequences are negative for us, and says that fMRI images

---

[*] Matthew D. Lieberman, *Social: Why Our Brains Are Wired to Connect* (New York: Crown, 2013), 84.

demonstrate that being altruistic activates the "reward system" in the brain and gives us pleasure.[*] Lieberman refutes the view expressed by Tocqueville that altruism is self-interest properly understood, a quid pro quo calculation that by helping others we are actually furthering our own interests. Instead, we practice altruism for its own sake, without the expectation of reward, because we are "built to take pleasure in cooperating and helping others."[†]

Lieberman attributes our brains' wiring to evolution. Throughout our development, we have survived individually when we have cooperated socially. By banding together in groups, our ancestors resisted threats to their survival that they could not have combated alone. So those who were most adept in making social connections were most likely to pass their genes on to their progeny. "Evolution is moving us ever closer to interdependent social living where we maximize what we can do together in groups."[‡] Lieberman speculates that altruism has its roots in the evolution of parental caregiving. Children of parents who care for them survive, while abandoned children do not.[§]

Lieberman reasons that because cooperation with

[*] Ibid., 86–92.
[†] Ibid., 91.
[‡] Ibid., 191.
[§] Ibid., 91.

others has been essential to survival, the capacity to harmonize one's self-interest with the interests of the group has been critical in our evolution. Individuals who prefer to go it alone have not survived the evolutionary process, while those who take on the mentality and behavior of the group live to convey to their children the ability to be social. In Lieberman's words, "We humans are built to be influenced by those around us, to follow their lead."* He adds that the social world tells us "what good people want and do." We are "built to soak all this up like a sponge."†

Lieberman often uses the same word to describe our brain's wiring; he speaks of how we are "built." We are built to be social. We are built to be altruistic. We are built to adapt our behavior to the standards of those around us. Lieberman writes as a scientist, but the similarity is striking between the word he uses, "built," and the word used in the first chapter of Genesis, "created." In science, humankind has been built over many millennia of gradual evolution. In Genesis, humankind was created by divine action in a day. Yet both science and scripture give similar accounts of what we are—our essential nature.

In Lieberman's analysis we are altruistic not because we calculate that it is in our self-interest to be so, but because that is the way we are wired. In Genesis, we humans

* Ibid., 195.
† Ibid., 235.

are more than simply good, we are "very good," because that's the way God made us. In science, our inherent altruism coexists with our self-interest. In Genesis, our goodness is corrupted by the archetype of self-interest, our desire to become like God. In science, we have evolved to conform to the influence of those around us. In Genesis, we are easily seduced by even the tiniest community, Eve and a serpent.

Genesis tells us that we are very good without telling us what that means except that God sees us that way. The New Testament demonstrates the meaning of good in the person of Christ, the "Second Adam." The first Adam became "a living being," the Second Adam "a life-giving spirit" (1 Corinthians 15:45). Comparing Adam and Christ, Paul says, "For just as by the one man's disobedience the many were made sinners, so by the one man's obedience the many will be made righteous" (Romans 5:19). In Philippians (2:8), Paul makes clear the meaning of obedience. Christ "became obedient to the point of death—even death on a cross." In Genesis our created nature is good. In the New Testament, the standard of good isn't the first Adam who yielded to the temptation of self-interest, but the Second Adam, the Christ and sacrificial love, the quintessence of altruism.

Few of us are obedient unto death, but all of us know people who, out of the depths of their faith, live lives of sacrificial love without any sense that what they do will somehow redound to their personal benefit. I'm thinking of my friends Sue and Phil Branson, who spend countless hours at a rescue mission helping the homeless, and Elaine and Steve Schleisman, who drive to a California desert community to mentor Hispanic children. Many faithful people do similar work, not to save their own souls, but to serve the needs of people who can never repay them.

This brings us to politics in its current state and how it dismisses the quality of altruism we are built/created to have. Politics is about the service of self and nothing else. It is about politicians who say and do anything to win the next election, pandering to the demands of constituents who believe that the main point of government is to serve their economic interests. With virtually no exceptions, politicians today never ask us to live for purposes beyond ourselves.

In today's politics, there is no upward lift, no inspiration, no call to the common good. Something essential is missing, something neuroscientists say we crave because of the way we are built, something the Bible teaches we are created to be, men and women who alongside our own interests care about the welfare of others.

I think that in our hearts we know that something essential is missing in the present state of politics. We see pandering for what it is. We believe that politics should be more than self-interest alone. So politics, with its exclusive attention to the self, disgusts us. It disgusts us that what is essential to how we are built, to how we are created, is so entirely missing, and that in its place there is so much meanness.

As presently practiced, politics will end up backfiring against its practitioners. Conservatives may think they will win support by self-righteousness toward gays and a hard line against immigrants. Liberals might think it to their advantage to tar their opponents with charges of homophobia and racism. But because we are built/created to care about and for other people, such tactics cannot long prevail. As a Republican, I think that the hard-edged meanness of some prominent members of our party will deservedly be our downfall unless we correct it.

Religion can supply what has gone missing: an understanding of what we humans are and an appeal to what we should be. We are more than the mean-spirited, egocentric chasers after our own interests that politicians and assorted media types take us for. We are created with a better nature that is revived and modeled for us in Christ. The work of faithful people is to spread this understanding.

Matthew Lieberman writes that "we humans are built to be influenced by those around us, to follow their lead." We know this to be true. What we are as parents, neighbors, teachers, coworkers, citizens, affects the behavior of those around us, and what they are affects us. Like us, our neighbors are both self-interested and altruistic. We have the capacity to influence them in one direction or the other. We can help bring out the best in people or the worst. The style of politics with its single-minded focus on self-interest brings out the worst. It could be the ministry of religious people to bring out the best if that's what we choose to do.

I witnessed an interesting if seemingly trivial example of how we influence one another when I was a young associate in a Wall Street law firm, and the City of New York had announced a crackdown on jaywalking. Wall Street types spanning a considerable range of ages saw the crackdown as the city's invitation to a game of red rover. Clusters of bankers, lawyers, and stock exchange employees hustled back and forth across lower Broadway close enough to helpless police officers to be seen and far enough away not to get caught. The city's effort to enforce the law turned into a brief, exuberant outbreak of anarchy. This was comical to watch, but it also offered a lesson. In America, the rule of law relies primarily on the willingness of the people to obey the law, and enforcement by the state is only effective when it is directed at a small percentage of the public who choose to be miscreants. For example, the collection of federal income taxes depends primarily on the willing if grudging reporting by taxpayers of what they owe, not on the threat that un-

derreporting may lead to fraud prosecution by government. If a lot of people want to break the law, they will do
so, and short of becoming a police state, government can
do little about it. A free society, that is, one where government is not monitoring our every move, requires citizens
who obey the law not for fear of being caught, but because obeying the rules is the right thing to do.

But how, other than by law, do we know how we are
supposed to behave? Who is to tell us what's the right
thing to do? Laughing jaywalkers on Broadway thought
that they were only having fun because by being part of a
pack they were assuring one another that taunting the
police was a way of having fun. Loudmouths at ballparks
think their obscenities are funny and acceptable behavior until someone tells them otherwise. The murderous
actions of German police officers in Poland told waver-
ing comrades that shooting Jews was the right thing to
do. In many countries, giving bribes to public officials is
common because for the public it is accepted practice.
We fall in with those around us, adopting for ourselves
the standards of our culture unless we hear some other
voice that tells us that our culture is wrong and that we
should take a stand and transform it.

Religion is that other voice. In prohibiting theft and
murder, it reinforces what the state does by enacting laws.
In some cases, the commands of religion exceed anything governmental authorities could legislate. "Thou

shalt not covet" is a commandment that will never be found in a statute. In other cases religion attempts to influence our conduct where the law has been powerless to do so. When sexuality devolves into promiscuity, religion is a more effective guide to conduct than is legislation. When the state is powerless as families fall apart, religion is better than the state in teaching the duty of parents to their children. Where new laws fail to deter sharp business practices, religion can better instruct us in fair dealing than can government.

When Jesus tells the rich young man to obey the commandments, he enumerates rules common to law and religion—don't murder, steal, or commit adultery—and in so doing, he moves us beyond fear of law enforcement to willing compliance with the norms of religion. He then goes much further than the standard rules of good behavior: "You shall love your neighbor as yourself." This is the Love Commandment, and it far exceeds anything that could be reduced to law.

When our first four presidents emphasized the virtue of citizens, they meant more than upright personal conduct. Most important in their minds was that Americans must be committed to the common good by placing the nation's interest above their own. For Alexis de Tocqueville and the creators of game theory, service to others was really an extension of self-interest. By helping you I will help myself. Today's politics undercuts the mutual understanding that we benefit from helping each other, and takes the opposite approach by dividing Americans between "us" and "them" and creating combat between competing interests in order to energize supporters. In President Obama's 2012 reelection campaign, the "them" was the wealthiest 1 percent of Americans. For Governor Romney, the "them" was the 47 percent who pay no federal income tax. Today, politics is a zero-sum game with candidates who pledge to help one group at the expense of another. The result of this divisive strategy is an extreme version of the party spirit George Washington warned against in his Farewell Address in which virtue, meaning commitment to the common good, collapses. Where then can America turn to recover its lost virtue? I believe that virtue, our willingness to serve more than our self-interest, should be the gift of religion to politics.

Religion is the counterweight to self-interest. It sets love of God and love of neighbor against love of self, and for Christians, it does so in the starkest and most absolute terms. There is nothing halfhearted about it. The standard by which Christians measure our love for each other is Christ's love for us to the point of his unimaginably awful death on the Cross.

Measured against that standard, you and I fall short. From time to time we learn of rare exceptions—a mother who risks her life by pushing her child out of the path of a car, a soldier who saves his comrades by throwing himself on top of a live grenade—but in the world in which we live, most of us do not love our neighbors as much as we love ourselves, much less love them enough to die for them. However, the fact that we do not live up to the standard of self-sacrifice is no excuse for dismissing its relevance to us. The Cross is still before us. The Cross shows us how we are supposed to live and who we are supposed to be.

Reinhold Niebuhr was a realist who understood that the Love Commandment could not be reduced to a political program. Politics is the art of compromise, and the Love Commandment is uncompromising. If we were to apply the absolute standard of the Cross to politics, the trade-offs that make politics workable would become impossible. Although the Love Commandment cannot be translated into a political program, it is relevant to you and me in how we live our lives, how we relate to other people, and, yes, how we approach politics. The Love Commandment is addressed to people, not programs. You and I are to love our neighbors as ourselves. This is a nondelegable responsibility. No political program can do our loving for us.

Niebuhr spoke of the Love Commandment in connection with the prophetic tradition. As the prophets of Israel confronted a disobedient people, so the Love Commandment confronts us in our selfishness:

> The prophetic tradition in Christianity must insist on the relevance of the ideal of love to the moral experience of mankind on every conceivable level.*

This is what Niebuhr called the "impossible possibility." He believed that while it is impossible for us to live up to Christ's standard of sacrificial love, that standard should be the measure of our morality "on every conceivable level."

No one has influenced how I think about the relationship between religion and politics more than Reinhold Niebuhr. That said, I don't find the expression "impossible possibility" very helpful. For me, to say that a standard for living is impossible is close to telling me, "Don't bother." Also, in commanding us to love one another, I don't think that God is asking of us something we can't do. I would rather think in terms of a scale; on one end, pure self-interest, on the other end, the Cross. The work of religion is to move us on the scale from pure self-interest toward the Cross, getting us as far as possible along the scale, but never quite reaching the Cross. Paul was realistic when he told the Philippians (2:4), "Let each of you look not only to his own interests, but also to the interests of others." Yes, we will always be looking to our

---

* Reinhold Niebuhr, *An Interpretation of Christian Ethics* (New York: Harper Brothers, 1935), 104.

own interests. That is the reality of life. It is the reality America's early statesmen built into our constitutional system when they created checks and balances. But virtue is moving beyond pure self-interest and looking to the interests of others. Politics pushes the scale heavily toward pure self-interest. Religion pushes the scale toward the interests of others. It tilts against interest groups focused solely on their own well-being. It counters the typical "What's in it for me?" with "What can I do for you?"

To an extent, the claim of the Love Commandment resembles the claim of patriotism. Both call us to live beyond ourselves in the service of interests greater than our own. There are many instances of people sacrificing themselves for the sake of the nation, especially at times of war. Nathan Hale's famous "I only regret that I have but one life to give for my country" is a prime expression of such self-sacrifice. But most of the time and for most of us, patriotism doesn't require self-sacrifice. It can exist perfectly well with the aggressive service of self-interest. We can feel quite patriotic when we recite the Pledge of Allegiance while being intensely focused on maximizing our own well-being. Indeed, we celebrate our country in large part for what it does for us, as it gives us the freedom to pursue our personal interests and realize our individual potential. Organizations like the American Legion and the Veterans of Foreign Wars proudly honor our flag while jealously protecting the benefits received by their members. Politicians who think of themselves as public servants, and rightly so, do what is necessary to get themselves elected. In sum, in our daily lives, self-interest and patriotism do not compete with each other; they co-exist.

But the Cross doesn't coexist with self-interest; it is its antithesis. Although seldom realized perfectly by sinful humankind, it pulls us out of our self-absorption, orienting us toward the kingdom of God. Unlike patriotism, the Christ of the Cross is more than even a very important part of life. Christ of the Cross is the way, the truth, and the life.

The prophetic insistence that we look beyond our own interests to the common good is directed to both politicians and their public. The message to politicians is quite simple: Be prepared to lose. I have heard politicians quote with approval Charlie Brown's comment in a *Peanuts* cartoon: "Winning isn't everything, but losing isn't anything." But in their hearts, I think they don't believe the first clause in that sentence. In their minds the worst imaginable fate is to lose an election. So, in pursuit of personal victory, anything goes. People who before they became candidates would never have thought of personally vilifying a competitor are unflinching in slinging any mud they can find and spending huge amounts of money to do so. Politicians who know that reckless fiscal policies will make America progressively weaker as we pass to future generations a legacy of massive debt have no problem promising voters whatever it takes to win their support. If winning and holding on to an office is the top priority, then why be troubled by the consequences for the nation? In *Profiles in Courage,* John F. Kennedy honored politicians who stood for the good of the country at the risk of their own careers. There are few profiles in courage around today, which is all the more reason for prophetic voices to ask politicians to risk defeat and to assure them that there can be honor in losing.

The prophetic message to the public is that America is greater than any of its parts, and that by demanding satisfaction of our own interests regardless of the cost, we are damaging the country. Yes, we all have our own interests, but if our single-minded concern is serving those interests and electing politicians who will pander to them, America has a very bleak future.

I do not think that the gift of religion to politics is the advocacy of any platform or any particular position on an issue. The gift of religion to politics is the insistence that we must serve interests that are greater than our own.

It may well be that our best efforts to live the Love Commandment don't produce the results we had hoped to achieve. That was the experience of some very good people from my hometown. Led by the energetic commitment of Debbie Smith, wife of the Episcopal bishop of

Missouri, our diocese has entered into a companion relationship with the Episcopal Diocese of Lui in South
Sudan, the newest country and one of the poorest in the
world. Describing South Sudan as poor or underdevel-
oped gives most Americans no idea of the reality. A decade or so ago, as President Bush's special envoy, I saw
the land up close, and learned that nothing there resembles anything we know in America, even in our very poorest communities. Absent what we call houses, Southern
Sudanese lived in huts made of sticks, often in tiny settlements connected to the rest of the country only by roads
so eroded as to be barely usable. Electricity and commu-
nications were generally absent, as was public health. I
saw an emaciated man walking on all fours (polio?). In
Rumbek, I saw a man squatting in the dust of a dirt road
making flip-flops out of a discarded tire. My guide told
me, "That is our shoe factory." South Sudan needs a lot
of help, and the Episcopal Diocese of Missouri is there to
help, building churches and schools and pitching in
where it can.

Getting there is at least a twenty-four-hour journey
from St. Louis that includes flying to Europe and taking
a connecting flight to Nairobi before setting out into the
interior of South Sudan. Once there, living conditions
for American volunteers are rudimentary. Despite the
difficulty, my fellow Episcopalians have made the effort
to go to Lui over and over again. When they arrived, they

brought with them their energy and goodwill, and they brought some money they had raised to give to the church at Lui. And then the money they had scraped together to use for this very needy cause was stolen. Of course, we don't know what happened to that money except that it didn't go to the worthy cause for which it was intended. Let's imagine that it wasn't simply grabbed by a thief. Let's imagine that instead of being used for a good cause it was diverted to some really evil cause. How do we think about such an event? How do we think about situations when good works don't work? It's an important question, because the failure of people who try to do good is not at all unusual. I know from firsthand experience in the same place where Missouri's Episcopalians have been at work, Sudan.

Sudan's civil war had been going on for more than two decades at a cost of two million lives when I became special envoy. What struck me soon after taking that job was the intense interest so many countries and parties had in advancing the cause of peace. Nations comprising the African Union, especially Kenya and Uganda, were engaged in the peace process, as were European countries led by Britain and Norway. That President Bush named me his special envoy demonstrated his personal commitment that extended well beyond an initial Rose Garden ceremony. I spoke with the president in person or by phone before every trip I made to the region. Members of Congress, notably Virginia's Frank Wolf, were keenly interested, as were various nongovernmental organizations. With America's presidency of the UN Security Council in November 2004, we organized a rare council meeting outside New York, taking all fifteen members to Nairobi to put pressure on the negotiations. All this international effort to help was effective. In January 2005, representatives of Sudan's government and the rebels signed a peace agreement in a sports stadium in Nairobi. The agreement provided for remaining a united country with shared leadership for five years, followed by a referendum in the south on whether to continue as a united Sudan or to form a separate country.

Sitting in that stadium on a brilliantly sunny day was one of the high points of my life. I thought that an enormous amount of attention and effort had paid off. After decades of bloodshed, at last there would be peace in Sudan. I believed that there was a will on both sides, strongly held by the south's great leader John Garang, to hold the country together, and that the future of a united Sudan was promising.

Then a separate civil war intensified in the western Darfur region of the country. A few months after the peace agreement, John Garang died in a plane crash, and the hope for a united country died with him. New fighting broke out in the long-contested middle of the country, and after five years, the people of the south overwhelmingly voted for separation. But that was not the end of the trail of disappointment. The new nation of South Sudan had trouble holding itself together as fighting broke out between competing Dinka and Nuer tribes. Certainly the good work of the many countries, individuals, and organizations was worthwhile in that it ended a terrible civil war and saved countless lives. But the euphoria we felt in that Nairobi stadium was short-lived. The potential we had hoped for wasn't realized, and Sudan is still a fractious place. Our best efforts had not worked as well as we had hoped.

Examples of our best efforts not working out as well as we intended abound in everyday life. We know teachers or volunteer mentors who find no reciprocal effort in their pupils. We give money to a beggar who spends it on drugs. We devote hours to licking envelopes for candidates hoping they are messiahs, and we find out they are scoundrels. So often do our best efforts lead to disappointment that there is a common phrase that describes the phenomenon: "No good deed goes unpunished." What is true for those who try to do good works in their daily lives is just as true for those who earnestly try to make the world better by influencing public policy. Did my two years of work to strengthen laws against employment discrimination actually advance the cause of civil rights? I'm not sure. Did all the work of all the people working for healthcare reform, and not just for Obamacare, really make people healthier? Maybe not. Are there unintended and undesirable consequences to our most well-meaning efforts? Very possibly so. It's easy to get carried away when we try to accomplish all these good things. And it's understandable when we cease bothering, give up, and turn in on ourselves. So why should we try to do good when our experience teaches us that often our good works don't work?

Religion's answer is that we bother to do good works because God made us just for that purpose. This is a lesson from the second chapter of Genesis. As Miroslav Volf points out, God created the earth and then entrusted humankind with making it fruitful. Volf argues that we are God's cocreators, and however seemingly insignificant and even failed our efforts may be, "God makes sure that none of what is true, good, and beautiful in our work will be lost. In God, everything that we have done in cooperation with God will be preserved."*

We are God's cocreators. That is a very profound concept meaning that all our efforts, however inadequate, have divine significance. A worker in construction may contribute very little, and the work may not be of the highest value. Still, however small, it is incorporated into the project. But to be God's cocreators is not to be God. Our contribution to creation is bound to be imperfect,

---

* Miroslav Volf, *A Public Faith: How Followers of Christ Should Serve the Common Good* (Grand Rapids, MI: Brazos Press, 2011), 35.

because we are imperfect. Keeping this in mind—in other words, maintaining a healthy degree of modesty— is especially important for those of us who do work that calls on us to compromise: politics. But to know that our efforts are imperfect and that the good we intend will often fall far short of what we can achieve is no excuse for not showing up on the job or not giving our work as God's cocreators our best efforts.

CHAPTER FOUR

ONE NATION

R obert Putnam's scholarly analysis of our growing separation from one another is borne out by our personal experience. Our isolated individualism contradicts our self-perception as one indivisible nation, undermines functioning government, and challenges religion at the congregational level to become a ministry of reconciliation.

As evidence of our growing isolation, consider a central room in American homes once known as the "parlor." It was a place for receiving visitors and exchanging talk. Now the word seems quaint. It became the "family room," a place where we could escape from the outside world and retreat to the bosom of the family. Then the family room became the "entertainment center," where the dominant sound isn't the voices of spouse and children but the TV, which asks for no personal interaction after we decide what program to watch. Politicians often refer to what families talk about "around the kitchen table." But for many of us either there is no kitchen table or no discussion around it—only the sound of television.

Occasionally on courthouse squares or in small-town city parks, one can still find a bandstand—a relic of the past when neighbors gathered in public places for shared entertainment. We can envision our ancestors in folding chairs or on blankets listening to the marches of John Philip Sousa. It's hard to imagine today, but there was a time when people actually enjoyed sitting through speeches, even by politicians. Sally's great-grandfather was a turn-of-the-twentieth-century Tennessee politician named Robert L. Taylor who after retiring from the U.S. Senate went on the lecture circuit, where he entertained crowds by making speeches and playing the fiddle. His oratory was flowery and witty. In one speech, he compared traveling salesmen to drummers climbing Jacob's Ladder to sell harps to angels. People loved it. It got them out of the house and brought them into company with their neighbors.

Today we need not leave the home for entertainment or for much else. Many of us can work from home, and we can homeschool our children. When we do leave the house, we can drive alone in our cars to the anonymity of shopping malls. If we go to the office, it may be more a place of individual effort than group enterprise.

A contemporary of mine has noted how the practice of law has changed over the last half century. He says that in his early years there was a lot of personal interaction within firms, with lawyers prowling the corridors, poking their heads into offices, and seeking informal advice from their colleagues. Now what he observes from the time he arrives in the morning until he leaves in the afternoon is the backs of the heads of young lawyers who are hunched over computer screens doing research on LexisNexis. The law library, once a common workspace, has been all but deserted for the more efficient and more isolating computer. One no longer need walk the corridors for face-to-face visits with one's colleagues. A much faster and effective way to solicit advice is to shoot the firm an email in which the request for help often begins with the words "Pardon the interruption." It is as though a momentary break in the isolated work of one's fellows is a barely tolerable bother for which one must seek pardon.

Even in our social life, we are less than social. Next time you are in a restaurant, notice the young couples who are presumably on dates. The ambience and the food may be perfect, but the company is not. Instead of gazing at each other, they are gazing at their iPhones. Instead of talking, they are texting.

The plight of the elderly represents an especially sad form of isolation. While serving in the Senate, I didn't do much in the parish ministry, but I tried to do something. We belonged to St. Alban's Church on the grounds of the Washington Cathedral. Our excellent rector, the Reverend Frank Wade, gave me just enough work to be useful, but not so much that I couldn't handle it consistent with my day job. I was responsible for celebrating Communion at the 7:30 service on Tuesday mornings and for taking Communion to shut-ins I tried to visit about once a month. The home visitations were depressing, but they were important because I was one of the few contacts the people I saw had with the world beyond their apartments.

The word "shut-ins" well describes the people I visited. They were shut into their apartments, unable to go to church. So my job was to bring the church to them. Almost all of them were women who had never been married or who had outlived their husbands. Children, if any, lived in faraway places and were seldom seen. Their friends were long gone, giving me the impression that when I completed my visit, the next person they would see would be me. The apartments were small and crammed with the belongings brought there from the far more spacious homes of their past. Housecleaning was minimal if any. I would try to clear a small table space for my Communion set, moving magazines and bric-a-brac to make room, and often found the sticky residue of some long-ago spilt substance. After the service, I would go to the kitchen to clean my small chalice and find the sink piled high with dirty dishes. It was clear that no one was caring for the shut-ins and they could not care for themselves.

A few of them had caregivers, which is a generous and inaccurate way to describe people who showed up for the sole purpose of collecting money for doing nothing. On one visit, an elderly lady sat on a small chair as I arranged the Communion set on a rickety table. Behind her was the caregiver, sprawled out on a sofa, the crook of an elbow covering her eyes, motionless from the minute I arrived until the minute I left. At least there was someone on the premises, I suppose. For eighteen years of visiting shut-ins, I had the impression that the façades of their apartment buildings hid something dreadful inside: a generation of elderly women, abandoned to their loneliness.

Our isolation from each other has consequences for our health. Over a decade, chronically lonely Americans over the age of forty-five increased from one in five to one in three. Between 1999 and 2010, the suicide rate for men in their fifties rose nearly 50 percent. According to Ross Douthat, "there's a strong link between suicide and weakened social ties" including "family obligations" and "civic and religious participation."[*]

More than its effect on our personal well-being, our increased isolation has had consequences for our life together, including our politics. A number of writers have

---

[*] Ross Douthat, "All the Lonely People," *New York Times,* May 18, 2013, citing Judith Shulevitz on chronic loneliness and Bruce Wilcox on suicide.

commented on this, all in the same vein. Robert Putnam has pointed out that as we have withdrawn from society, we have become increasingly distrustful of one another.* This makes sense, as we are more likely to trust people we know than strangers.

Commenting on national security leaker Edward Snowden, David Brooks speaks of "the atomization of society, the loosening of social bonds," and notes "the rising tide of distrust, the corrosive spread of cynicism, the fraying of the social fabric and the rise of people who are so individualistic in their outlook that they have no real understanding of how to knit others together and look after the common good."†

Many have speculated about the causes of our recent political dysfunction, blaming it on talk radio, twenty-four-hour news channels, or gerrymandered legislative districts. There is likely some truth in each of these theories, but it seems to me that another possibility deserves attention. Robert Putnam makes a strong case that the shift from social engagement to individualistic isolation took place during the last third of the twentieth century. I noticed the beginning of a change in the Senate from a relative degree of collegiality and cooperation to combativeness and polarization after the 1992 election. My sup-

---

* Robert Putnam, *Bowling Alone: The Collapse and Revival of American Community* (New York: Simon & Schuster, 2000), chapter 8.
† David Brooks, "The Solitary Leaker," *New York Times,* June 10, 2013.

position has been that the change originated with the arrival in the Senate of new members who had previously served in the more rough-and-tumble House of Representatives. Now I suspect that the roots of dysfunction are deeper and more far-reaching than one election cycle, or even than more bombastic media and safer congressional districts. I now suspect that there is a relationship between the social breakdown noted by Putnam and the political breakdown of today. It is plausible that what is happening in politics is the consequence of what has happened in society.

Politics is a collective activity. It begins, as the Preamble of the Constitution proclaims, as a coming together of a "people," with all their differences, "to form a more perfect union." It includes the periodic coming together of the people at elections to choose their representatives. It requires the allegiance of the people to their constitutional system and compliance with the rule of law. It is complex, functioning at federal, state, and local levels through three branches with separate powers. Because government is complex, its successful operation depends on a high degree of cooperation from a host of participants, many of whom have the power, if they choose to exercise it, to be obstructive. When the U.S. Senate functions effectively, it does so by unanimous consent. Each senator has the right to block progress on legislation by uttering two words—"I object"—to motions to proceed.

So forbearance by all senators in the assertion of individual power is the necessary condition of the Senate's daily activities. The capacity of individuals to be a people is the condition of being a nation. The willingness of individual politicians to function as a whole is the condition of a workable government.

To the extent that we disengage from society and retreat into isolated individualism, we cease being a people. Our concern is no longer for the whole but for the self. The question we ask of every situation is, "What's in it for me?" This is the question politicians are hearing from every quarter. Ask not what I can do for the country; ask what the country can do for me. Politics becomes the assertion of individual rights and the pandering to individual demands.

A marked change in political discourse has followed the shift from social connectedness to isolation. I don't want to suggest that all was sweetness and light when, as a senator, I hosted town hall meetings with constituents. Many of the people who showed up at those events had serious complaints about something I had done. At one contentious meeting five miles from a dioxin site just outside St. Louis, everyone was mad. Some protested that the government had bought out their neighbors but not them. Those who had been bought out argued that the government hadn't paid them enough. A third group said that any payout to anyone was a rip-off of taxpayers.

Protestors were holding signs. One person wore a mock space suit. I thought it was quite an uproar, but these days, political forums are often mob scenes where crowds shout down and sometimes threaten politicians. True discourse requires mutual respect. Where there is no mutuality, no sense that despite our differences we are in this together, there is no respect for contrary opinions. Politics becomes a shouting match where the loudest side wins.

Then there are the television talk shows with helpless moderators and advocates for competing positions who talk over and through each other. There is never the sense that the participants are seeking some point of agreement, some common ground, some consideration of the opposing view. The idea is to so dominate discussion as to drown out the other side.

The expression "My way or the highway" accurately describes today's politics. It applies to the public, the pundits, and the politicians. Unlike Russell Long, whose method was to accommodate every member of the Finance Committee by giving each a stake in the legislation, the prevailing method is to block action on everything until the opposition capitulates. So we have the spectacle of one senator holding the floor for a full day or threatening to block confirmation of presidential nominees until his extraneous demand is satisfied. When one is isolated with no allegiance to the whole, when all that counts is oneself, then democracy—government of, by, and for the people—breaks down.

In *Who Are We?* Harvard's Samuel Huntington argued that an influx of immigrants since 1965 plus bilingualism have undermined America's cultural identity and turned us into a hodgepodge of what he calls "ampersands," hyphenated Americans celebrating different countries and speaking different languages. To the contrary, my experience is that we share a common pride in our country that is not related to our national wealth, our standard of living, our strong military, or large corporations or great universities, although we could boast of all of that. Other countries are wealthy and have high standards of living. Even with a strong military, we are vulnerable in a time of terror, and only 9 percent of our people think that the United States should be the single world leader.[*] Great corporations are not all American, and those that are are multinational. While our universities are excellent, our educational system overall lags behind many countries. These standard markers of a nation's success tell us that America is doing well, even very well, relative to the rest of the world, but none of them marks America as exceptional.

How about our culture? We export our movies and

[*] Pew Research Center, "U.S. Public, Experts Differ on China Policies," September 18, 2012, http://www.pewglobal.org/2012/09/18/u-s-public -experts-differ-on-china-policies/.

music, but only 49 percent of Americans believe that our culture is superior to others, down from 60 percent in 2002. The number is even lower (37 percent) among the eighteen- to twenty-nine-year age group, a leading consumer of pop entertainment.[*]

More than the citizens of any other country, Americans are a proud people. In a 2008 Pew Global Attitudes Project survey, 78 percent of American respondents said they are "very proud of their nationality." That compares with 44 percent of Spaniards, our closest rivals among Western European countries polled.[†] That's a baseline percentage. Seventy-eight percent of us are "very proud" in normal times, and when special events occur, when Navy SEALs kill Osama bin Laden or when our athletes win an Olympic competition, our pride peaks even higher.

I saw this on a sunny afternoon in June 2004 when it was my privilege to accompany Ronald Reagan's body in a motorcade from Naval Base Ventura County to its final resting place at the Reagan Presidential Library in Simi Valley, California. It was a long, meandering route that allowed the tens of thousands who turned out to pay their respects to catch a momentary glimpse of the hearse

[*] Pew Research Center, "The American–Western European Values Gap," November 17, 2011, http://www.pewglobal.org/2011/11/17/the-american-western-european-values-gap/#survey-report.
[†] Pew Research Center, Global Attitudes Survey, Spring 2008, http://www.pewglobal.org/question-search/?qid=436&cntIDs=&stdIDs=.

that carried the former president. In places, the crowds were five or more deep, with children standing at the front holding handmade signs saying, "Thank you, Mr. President." On highway overpasses, hook-and-ladder fire trucks held aloft American flags, and at intersections police officers standing straight as West Point cadets smartly saluted the passing hearse. Many in the crowd held small American flags, and nearly all pressed their right hands to their hearts. There was no doubt how they felt on that magnificent day of national unity. They were one people, they were Americans, and they were proud. They were a mix of races and ethnicities who would not have agreed with Samuel Huntington's thought that we are a hodge-podge of ampersands. By their presence, they were saying quite the opposite, that America stands for important values, that each of us is a part of a greater whole, that we share a bond with one another.

At times of disaster—9/11 is the prime example—there are surges of patriotism as Americans sense that we need to pull together. After terrorists flew planes into our buildings and into a Pennsylvania field, we added "God Bless America" to "Take Me Out to the Ballgame" during the seventh-inning stretch. Days after an EF5 tornado cut a seven-mile-long path through the center of Joplin, Missouri, killing 160 people and flattening every building in its way, I visited the ruins of what had been homes and churches to find that citizens had planted American flags amid the rubble. When all was lost, it was important to make a statement: We are Americans.

Many people warn us, with much justification, that our pride in country can be dangerous and can lead us in the wrong direction. The misplaced belief that God has given us a special commission to push our weight around and impose our values on other cultures tells the world that we are arrogant. It may result in tragic military commitments. This warning should always be in our minds as should a modesty in how we present ourselves to others. That said, most of us are convinced, and rightly so, that America is indeed exceptional, that it is more than a place where we happen to live.

In sum, Americans are proud that, with all our differences, we share a common bond, and they long for the bond to be strong. That longing converges with what can be the mission of the faithful: the ministry of reconciliation.

When considering a ministry of reconciliation, a good place to begin is Matthew 5:23–24:

> So when you are offering your gift at the altar, if you remember that your brother or sister has something against you, leave your gift there before the altar and go; first be reconciled to your brother or sister, and then come and offer your gift.

These verses from the Sermon on the Mount make two points: first, that what we do in relationship to other people takes precedence over sacerdotal religion; second, that the work we are supposed to do with other people is reconciliation. Being connected with our brothers and sisters is our first obligation, formal worship is secondary.

My friend Bishop Hays Rockwell gave me excellent advice as I once prepared to conduct the funeral of an exemplary person who was not a practicing Christian. Rockwell said that how a person lives is more important than what creed he confesses. I agree, not because I denigrate the importance of theology. I do not. It's important to understand and articulate church doctrine and to make clear what it does not include. At the same time, I can't imagine that when God holds us accountable for our lives we are given a theological exam. Once I read the New Testament using highlighters of several colors to mark those passages about what we believe and those about how we live. The latter were the more numerous, by far.

In the Great Commission at the end of Matthew's Gospel, the risen Lord tells his followers to "make disciples of all nations." I don't think that the best way to make disciples is by force of argument. As a young man, I tried to argue with people about religion, with the discussion getting absolutely nowhere. What is essentially a matter of faith turned into an exercise in showing off how very smart we were in pushing the other person into some intellectual corner. We confused religion with sophistry. The best way I know to make disciples is by example. We should be living advertisements for what it is like to be faithful people so that others want to imitate what we are, if not what we think. To live as a disciple is to win disciples, and in the Gospels the way to live as a disciple is by love. In John's Gospel (13:35), Jesus put this very clearly: "By this everyone will know that you are my disciples, if you have love for one another."

Paul added an important tactic to the strategy of winning disciples. We should be sympathetic to where others are in their own faith, and we should ingratiate ourselves with them. Suppose, he asked, we are with people whose faith is so weak that they fear that food in front of them has been offered to idols. Under those circumstances should Christians refrain from eating that food? Paul reasoned that since idols have no real existence it makes no difference what believers eat. But if their companions still harbor some residual belief in idols, then Christians should avoid eating the food lest by doing so they would weaken the belief of those who are less mature in their faith. What we do in witnessing our faith should be influenced by how our actions appear to others (1 Corinthians 8).

Paul then became more explicit. He said that he adjusted how he presented his beliefs in order to appeal to his audience and therefore win them to the Gospel. He lived as a Jew when he was with Jews. He was prepared to live either as someone who was under religious law or as someone who was not under religious law, depending on his company. "I have become all things to all people, that I might by all means save some. I do it all for the sake of the Gospel" (1 Corinthians 9:19–23).

Religion can be ingratiating or it can be off-putting, and it's clear that "for the sake of the Gospel," Paul preferred the former, and that he was prepared to go to great ends to accommodate the sensitivities and the beliefs of other people. The alternative is for religion to be off-putting, often intentionally so, by treating outsiders as though they are beyond redemption and not deserving of equal status with the true believers. Churches that practice closed Communion do this reasoning that the Eucharist is a sign of unity not shared with outsiders and that those who receive the sacrament "without discerning the body eat and drink judgment against themselves" (1 Corinthians 11:29). I once participated in an interfaith wedding in a Roman Catholic church; the bride was Catholic, the groom Protestant. The priest celebrated the Eucharist and proceeded to administer the sacrament to the bride but not the groom. The bride's side of the church rose and went to the altar. The groom's side remained in their pews. If the priest truly thought that the groom and his family were not worthy to receive the sacrament, why was it necessary for him to go out of his way to tell them so? Why not have had a mass for the bride and her family, say on the morning of the wedding, and then a simple exchange of vows where all present would be treated equally? Paul, who was sensitive to the residual feelings of former idol worshippers, would not have treated one group of faithful people as though they didn't belong. Nor would Jesus, who shared the Last Supper with Judas.

A second way religion can be off-putting is by picking fights. This it does when it emphasizes issues it knows are divisive. Robert Putnam and David Campbell argue in *American Grace* that religion is a source of societal divisions because of two issues, abortion and homosexuality. Absent those issues, they say, finding common ground in America would be more likely.*

It is one thing to have a religious position on divisive issues. It is quite another matter to harp on those issues. Paul certainly had strong positions on idolatry as well as on the subject of law versus grace. But in order to ingratiate himself and the faith he proclaimed with his audience, he was willing to finesse these differences for the sake of the Gospel. For him, it was a decision to use the best tactics in order to win over his listeners.

* Robert Putnam and David Campbell, *American Grace: How Religion Divides and Unites Us* (New York: Simon & Schuster, 2010), 310, 401.

Since positions against abortion and gay marriage are political losers, championing them serves no practical political objective. No matter how ardently opponents try to argue these questions, they will not succeed in changing four decades of jurisprudence on abortion or rapidly developing public opinion on gay marriage. They will lose adherents to religion, and they will make finding common ground difficult. If reconciliation is a principal value of religion, as I believe it is, then I would advise dropping abortion and gay marriage as salient political positions.

The least religious organizations can do to hold us together is to avoid driving us apart. But the work of reconciling religion is more than avoiding driving people away, and that work is done where the community of the faithful gather: in congregations. If they choose, and if they try, congregations can have a positive role in bringing us together and bridging what divides us.

For starters, congregations can make a greater effort to be communities of the faithful. That is, they can be more than places where people go for an hour or so and then depart. They can be gathering places where people get to know one another, perhaps in Bible study groups or food ministries, perhaps in social events such as card parties or what is an annual event at my church, a fund-raising "concert under the stars." You have a building; put it to use. Putnam and Campbell point out that people who are connected through religiously based social networks are more likely than others to be connected with the broader community. They are more likely to exhibit beyond their church groups qualities of neighborliness, engagement, and altruism. This correlation between social networking within congregations and connectedness beyond the congregation is independent of what is preached from the pulpit or believed as theological doctrine. Merely having friends in church is associated with being engaged beyond the church. Although Putnam and Campbell say that they cannot prove that the correlation they report is causal, they state that evidence suggests that it is. Churches where people are friends have societal impacts far beyond the walls of their buildings.

The work of making congregations into communities is made more difficult by the automobile. Today, people can drive great distances to the church of their choice, so they may have no contact with other members beyond church life. For most of us, the model of the parish church, where friends from the neighborhood see each other at worship, is a thing of the past. Also, as Bill Bishop points out in *The Big Sort,* when people can travel many miles to church, they can choose places where members think just as they think and where preachers tell them what they want to hear. The result is that instead of holding together people with diverse opinions, churches can be causes of our segmentation where we sort ourselves into like-minded groupings. A ministry of reconciliation bridges what separates us from one another. It does not provide enclaves where we can be safe from those who think differently than we do.

In addition to creating social networks within congregations, religious organizations can and do find creative ways to relate to the wider world. There are both informal and structural ways to do this. In *To Heal a Fractured World,* Rabbi Jonathan Sacks tells of an initiative in the United Kingdom that called on faith communities to do acts of kindness for people of different faiths. Such an initiative demands little or no formal structure, but it does require attentiveness by people who are on the lookout for opportunities where they can act. Some years ago, an excellent example occurred in my hometown of St. Louis. The Interfaith Partnership was operating a Meals on Wheels program delivering food to shut-ins when a day of expected activity coincided with Christmas. The mosques in St. Louis stepped forward and volunteered to do all the food delivery that day so that Christians could enjoy the holiday with their families. It was indeed an act of kindness that conveyed a clear message that religion is about caring for and connecting with people with different beliefs.

Shortly after two Muslim brothers detonated bombs near the finish line of the Boston Marathon, an article appeared in *The Wall Street Journal* describing the experience of a Bosnian family that had immigrated to the United States. Among various acts of kindness, the Muslim family stayed four months with a Methodist minister, received a free cancer operation from a Jewish doctor, and free dental care from a Protestant orthodontist.[*]

The deepest and most persistent division in America remains, as it has always been, racial. This was underscored when the fatal shooting of eighteen-year-old Michael Brown by Ferguson police officer Darren Wilson made my hometown the center of national, even international attention to the issue of racial disparities. Many religious leaders from St. Louis and around the country felt compelled by their faith to respond to a crisis now commonly referred to as "Ferguson." Church buildings became centers for gathering protestors. In a well-covered media event, clergy marched on the town's police station to confront officers with demands for individual repentance. From pre–Civil War preachers of emancipation through Dr. Martin Luther King Jr. to the present day, religious leaders have led the cause for racial justice. A ministry of reconciliation must continue that leadership, beginning with a recognition of where America now stands.

1. The economic inequality of black and white Americans is beyond dispute. In 2012, the median income of

---

[*] Kenan Trebincevic, "Two Muslim Brothers Who Took the Assimilation Path," *Wall Street Journal,* April 27, 2013.

black households was 58.44 percent of the median income of white households.[*] Between 2007 and 2011, 25.8 percent of African Americans lived in poverty, compared to 11.6 percent of whites.[†]

2. African Americans live in neighborhoods and attend schools where they are separate from whites. In our ten most segregated cities, including New York, Chicago, Los Angeles, Cleveland, and Philadelphia, 73.7 percent of African Americans live in segregated neighborhoods.[‡] Seventy-four percent of black students attend schools where the majority of students are not white. Thirty-eight percent of black students attend schools where 10 percent or less of students are white.[§]

3. The prospects of African-American children are bleak, especially in an economy that demands an increasingly well-educated workforce. In 2011, 67.8 percent

[*] U.S. Census Bureau, Current Population Survey, 1968–2013 Annual Social and Economic Supplements.

[†] Suzanne Macartney, Alemayehu Bishaw, and Kayla Fontenot, "American Community Survey Briefs"; U.S. Census Bureau, "Poverty Rates for Selected Detailed Race and Hispanic Groups by State and Place: 2007–2011," February 2013.

[‡] William H. Frey, "New Racial Segregation Measures for States and Large Metropolitan Areas: Analysis of the 2005–2009 American Community Survey," Brookings Institution with the University of Michigan Social Science Data Analysis Network, 2010.

[§] Gary Orfield, John Kucsera, and Genevieve Siegel-Hawley, *E Pluribus . . . Separation: Deepening Double Segregation for More Students,* Civil Rights Project report, September 19, 2012.

of black births were out of wedlock.[*] The math and reading skills of black high school seniors are at the same level as those of thirteen-year-old white students.[†]

4. The psychological gulf between African Americans and whites is as wide as the statistical differences. After the acquittal of George Zimmerman for the killing of Trayvon Martin, commentator Gary Younge asked whether the verdict meant that it was "open season on black boys after dark."[‡] Response to the Michael Brown killing varied sharply by race, with African Americans assuming that the police shot an unarmed teenager in cold blood while most whites thought that Officer Wilson was justified in protecting himself. The black reaction spanned social and economic distinctions. One very successful black attorney told me that every African-American professional he knows is convinced that the shooting of Brown was malicious. The assumption that blacks are targeted by white police is based on a long history of confrontations between police and citizens. Even black police officers recount experiences from their past where they were abused by white po-

[*] Rachel M. Shattuck and Rose M. Kreider, "Social and Economic Characteristics of Currently Unmarried Women with a Recent Birth: 2011," American Community Survey Reports, U.S. Census Bureau, May 2013.

[†] Kati Haycock, "Raising Achievement and Closing Gaps Between Groups: Lessons from School Districts on the Performance Frontier," Nevada Association of School Boards, Education Trust, November 19, 2011.

[‡] Gary Younge, *Guardian*, July 14, 2013.

lice. African Americans are convinced that they are harassed, disrespected, and unfairly arrested by police who consider their lives worthless and are ready to shoot them on sight. As a result of this widespread opinion, the reaction in Ferguson was to assume the guilt of Officer Wilson and demand that he be prosecuted. Law enforcement's response to Ferguson demonstrations included wearing riot gear and brandishing assault weapons atop military vehicles and served as further evidence to blacks that police were their enemies.

As was true in the aftermath of Waco, the belief that the police are a violent enemy undermines the ground on which a decent society must stand. Distrust can easily become disrespect for law, which can then progress to the sort of lawlessness that marred the demonstrations in Ferguson. If we are to have peace, it should be the goal of all of us to create a system of law enforcement that merits, and therefore receives, the trust of all citizens. The goal should be that African Americans believe they are treated fairly because they *are* treated fairly. The clergy march on the Ferguson police station was important as a statement of religious solidarity with a disadvantaged and historically abused minority, and it was squarely in the biblical tradition of standing with suffering people. By reaching out to a group that feels estranged from the rest of society, members of the clergy faithfully exercised their ministry. However, this was an instance when a more pastoral approach would have better served the cause of justice than the confrontational demand that individual police officers repent.

Were society hopelessly unjust, then prophetic confrontation without more would be an appropriate response. But society is not hopelessly unjust. There are so many good people who want to do the right thing—average citizens, including police officers—that it is worth appealing to their goodness. This, especially, should be the work of faithful people who are given the ministry of reconciliation. They can bring us together by guiding us toward what we can do together.

Since the death of Michael Brown, St. Louisans have been at work developing specific plans to increase public trust in law enforcement. The plans have included ways to increase African-American membership in police departments, improved training, police outreach to communities, and greater use of body cameras by police officers. Because traffic stops are a constant cause of friction, limiting speed traps as sources of municipal revenue would improve police-community relations. Such reforms promise real progress in racial justice, and those who are working to bring them to reality deserve the encouragement of ministers of reconciliation.

. . .

Beyond improving police practices, religious bodies and faithful people can do much to improve opportunities for African Americans. Catholic churches have long seen their parish schools as providing education to often underprivileged children who need not be Catholic. I am very proud of my nephew Donald Danforth III for founding and operating an elementary school that serves African-American children in St. Louis. My daughter Mary Stillman is starting a charter school for girls in North St. Louis. If we use our imaginations and make the effort, there are all kinds of concrete ways we can translate our religious motivation into action. I have been involved in two interfaith efforts in St. Louis that marshaled congregational resources to reduce racial disparities. Neither worked out as well as I had hoped, but they are useful lessons for the future. The first was named InterACT–St. Louis; the second, Faith Beyond Walls.

When I retired from the Senate in January 1995, I had some funds left over from my last campaign that I could spend for charitable purposes. Also, Dick Mahoney, who at the time was CEO of Monsanto, was good enough to organize an appreciation dinner to mark the end of my years in public office. Adding the two sources of funds, I transferred something in excess of $1 million to a newly formed organization, InterACT. Our mission was to form interfaith pairings of black and white congregations that would provide after-school mentoring for inner-city children. Our model was the successful work being done by Central Reform Congregation and its African-American partner, Cote Brilliante Presbyterian Church. In my mind, the creation of such pairings would serve four important purposes. First, it would strengthen congregations, which I think are the heart of religious life. Second, it would create opportunities for congregations to work together across faith lines. Third, it would involve white and black St. Louisans working together for a shared purpose. Finally, it would provide enrichment for disadvantaged children.

InterACT got off to a magnificent start. I recruited a top-flight board of directors, including the Reverend William Gillespie, pastor of Cote Brilliante Presbyterian Church; Archbishop (now Cardinal) Justin Rigali; and Jeff Stiffman, rabbi of Congregation Shaare Emeth. We hired an outstanding executive director, my former Senate staffer Ron Jackson, and we got to work forming partnerships. Two of the early pairings were St. Francis Xavier, the Jesuit college church of St. Louis University, with Washington Tabernacle Baptist Church, and predominantly black St. Alphonsus Rock Church with Congregation Shaare Emeth. Soon, InterACT had recruited twenty-six congregations and served about four hundred children.

It proved much easier to ignite initial enthusiasm for InterACT than to sustain it, and after a few years of success, the program died out. As Ron Jackson describes the cause of its demise, InterACT was built on the commitment of individual pastors and volunteers, but in most cases it did not become part of the ongoing mission of the congregations. Pastors and volunteers move on, and absent their personal dedication, the program disappears. Some pastors are more interested in getting people to come through their church doors than in providing outreach to nonmembers. I would add my own thought that InterACT was too complicated and tried to serve too many purposes. Perhaps it would have lasted longer if it had confined its efforts to recruiting mentors and not involved the more complicated work of forming partnerships across faith and racial lines.

The energy created by the visit of Pope John Paul II to St. Louis in January 1999 was the opportunity for my second interfaith/interracial initiative, Faith Beyond Walls. The idea was for congregations to act as hiring halls for volunteers. Specifically, I envisioned a ready response team should hateful incidents occur in St. Louis. Say there were a Klan march in one part of town; with a roster of willing people in hand, we could turn out ten times as many people for a simultaneous religious service of reconciliation in a different location. Or if vandals were to desecrate a Jewish site, we could within hours produce Christians with scrub brushes to clean up the mess.

As with InterACT, Faith Beyond Walls was off to a great start. The Reverend B. T. Rice, head of the African American Clergy Coalition, and Rabbi Mark Shook, chair of the Interfaith Partnership, presented the pope with a banner bearing our new logo. Well over two hundred people, half black, half white, showed up for the first day's project of painting large maps of the United States and the world on playgrounds of city schools. Subsequent work included the installation of inner-city playgrounds and the rebuilding of housing to accommodate victims of Hurricane Katrina who had moved to St. Louis.

Like InterACT, Faith Beyond Walls had excellent early leadership, first Marylen Stansbery, then Orvin Kimbrough, but leadership changed, funding dried up, and in 2007 it merged with the Interfaith Partnership. It now exists in name only, and is another example of a good idea that starts out strong and soon fizzles.

I still believe in all the purposes we hoped to serve in InterACT and Faith Beyond Walls. I believe in the critical importance of congregations in crossing barriers of faith and race. I believe that racial inequality is an even more pressing problem as higher levels of skill are required of our workforce. And I believe that this critical problem requires our affirmative attention and action, starting with our religious congregations. It will not be enough for people of faith to write Congress and tell someone else what to do. And in our efforts to do good, we should learn from our mistakes.

Here are the lessons I have learned from InterACT and Faith Beyond Walls:

1. It is easier to start something than to see it through for the long run.
2. Sustained energy more likely comes from within congregations than from outside organizations.
3. Pastors and volunteers come and go, and their enthusiasms come and go with them. If outreach is to last, it must be central to the mission of the congregation.

Having failed with two ideas about religion and race, I am going to offer two more ideas, realizing that if they ever got off the ground, they too would fade unless we have learned the above lessons.

The first idea came to me from Hank Webber, executive vice chancellor of Washington University in St. Louis and senior lecturer at its George Warren Brown School of Social Work. He suggests that congregations that are relatively well-off create one-to-one partnerships with inner-city churches with the goal of turning the poorer churches into community resources for their neighborhoods. Many churches have physical facilities including gathering spaces, classrooms, and even gymnasiums. With a little outside support, Webber believes they could become anchors for their communities, sponsoring recreational activities such as Little League teams for children and providing meeting space for civic groups. It could be a mission for a well-to-do congregation to support community activities in inner-city churches, and it could be a mission of inner-city churches to be community centers for their neighborhoods.

It isn't uncommon for religious bodies to form companion relationships with counterparts in distant countries. There is no reason why a parish church in St. Louis County couldn't form a companion relationship with an inner-city church in predominantly African-American North St. Louis. The positive results of such a relationship could be several and substantive: wholesome activities for kids, increased interaction among neighborhoods, and a stronger role for the church in its neighborhood.

The second idea is that relatively affluent congregations attempt to reduce the physical isolation of inner-city residents from the rest of the community, specifically by offering transportation to places of employment. A recent study by professors from Harvard and University of California at Berkeley points out the substantial variation in upward economic mobility among different American cities. The study notes that "high upward mobility areas tended to have higher fractions of religious individuals and fewer children raised by single parents." That would suggest a good reason for strengthening inner-city churches. The study also finds a "significant correlation" between income inequality and economic and racial residential segregation.[*] This finding stands to reason. When people are physically cut off from opportunity, they have little chance to be upwardly mobile. If a job opening is ten miles from the home of a potential applicant who has no car, and if public transportation is difficult, one's prospects for success are dim. Perhaps it would be possible for churches to fill the need of improving the physical mobility of the poor, and thereby economic mobility. Many churches have buses to take members to and from worship. Maybe the same buses could take inner-city residents to and from work. I'm not at all sure that this is a practical idea. But when churches see that it is their work to overcome isolation and create connections, they will find ways to do that.

The aspiration to overcome social barriers is an American value and a religious value. Equality as a principle was enshrined in the Declaration of Independence, even though slavery persisted nearly a century after its signing. Equality under the law was written into the Constitution in the Fourteenth Amendment, even though women could not vote for half a century after the amendment's

---

[*] Raj Chetty et al., "The Equality of Opportunity Project," Summary of Project Findings, July 2013.

ratification. The work of dismantling legal barriers is work in progress, as is the work of dismantling barriers we create in our attitudes toward one another. Unlike our British antecedents with their titles of nobility, we are a classless country. That doesn't mean that we have the same wealth or income or lifestyle. It does mean that no one should be consigned by birth to an unchangeable circumstance. All of us should have a chance to move upward, and all of us should behave toward one another as though we are equals. That is why each of us has a responsibility to make us in fact that one nation we aspire to be in principle. As a practical matter, much of the work of opening opportunities for the have-nots must be done by the haves, and this is where religion will take the lead. Robert Putnam and David Campbell have noted the correlation between religious networking and class bridging:

> Among the American upper classes, those who are religiously observant are more likely to report friendship and social interaction with people on welfare or manual workers than comparably placed secular Americans.[*]

While Putnam and Campbell attribute social bridge building to church attendance rather than church teach-

[*] Putnam and Campbell, *American Grace*, 253.

ing, it is consistent with the words of Saint Paul, "Do not be haughty, but associate with the lowly" (Romans 12:16). The benefits of social bridge building run in two directions. Those who are well-off can give material support to those who are not, and in giving they can receive much in return. This is especially true when two-way bridge building is the ministry of religious congregations. Financially marginal congregations have lessons to teach their well-endowed partners about generosity in giving, social outreach, and caring for members of the church family. Bridge building is a mutual enterprise with mutual rewards.

CHAPTER FIVE

CREATION

The magnificent Frederick Hart sculpture over the main door of the Washington National Cathedral is titled *Ex Nihilo* (*Out of Nothing*). The subject is the Creation, which in theology is ex nihilo—that is, there was no independent existence from which God created the universe, there was nothing at all. But it's hard to think about nothing, and it's impossible to portray it artistically. So in Hart's sculpture the torsos and limbs of men and women are represented as emerging from an oceanlike background. Form emerges from formlessness, but not from nothing, and creation consists of bringing order out of chaos.

While theologians would not recognize chaos as a physical state that preexisted God's initial act of creation, it is clear from Genesis that creation consisted of setting limits and establishing order. So God separated day from night and land from water. At each step of this ordering of the universe, God saw that his work was good. The message of Genesis is that God's work brings order out of chaos, and God's ordering work is good. Because we humans are God's cocreators, tilling and keeping God's garden (Genesis 2:15), we are partners in bringing order out of chaos. Our original sin was refusing to honor the limits God had created and rebelling against the God-given order.

It would go way too far to claim that order is always good. Totalitarian regimes are masters at establishing order at the cost of freedom—it was said that Mussolini made the trains run on time. However, to acknowledge that some systems for creating order are evil does not mean that chaos is good. God's work brings order out of chaos, and America's work creates a system that is both orderly and just. That work began with the writing of our Constitution, and it continues under our system of law.

A dictionary definition of chaos is "a state of utter confusion and disorder,"* and it accurately describes the chaotic state of American politics, especially at the federal level. The best example of the current chaos is the recurring habit of lurching from crisis to crisis regarding the debt ceiling and funding the government. Repeatedly, Republicans in Congress threaten to prevent an increase of the authorized level of the national debt or to shut down government unless the president meets their

---

* *Shorter Oxford English Dictionary,* 5th ed. (2003).

policy demands. Repeatedly the president responds that he will not negotiate with a gun to his head. Breathless commentators take to the air with dire predictions of doom. They warn us that the United States will go into default, that our credit rating will fall, that the doors of government will close and Social Security checks will not be issued. Adding to the recurring dramas of the debt limit and funding government, there are more targeted uncertainties aimed at groups of individuals and businesses. From 1997 to 2015, the way in which government compensated physicians was set one year at a time. To create an artificially rosy picture of out-year budgeting, the tax credit for business spending on research and development is extended for increments of a year with no guarantee that research-focused businesses can count on its future availability. It is as though the intent of Congress is to keep America perpetually off balance.

Many businesspeople tell me that they can adjust to anything government will do so long as they know what it is. With regard to research and development, they say that their planning should be long-term, and not based on tax provisions that may or may not exist a year or two hence, yet the message from Congress is that business cannot count on today's tax incentives. Hospital administrators say much the same thing. It's impossible to plan for the future when government is constantly changing the rules.

Unpredictability is especially acute when rules are made and then changed by executive order. At least Congress is slow-moving, and the legislation it enacts takes time and gives warning. By contrast, the executive branch can change direction quickly—witness the sudden announcement of delays in enforcing the employer mandate in the Affordable Care Act.

Our constitutional system provides an orderly process for deciding how government relates to the American people. Schoolchildren learn this process as they watch cartoon characters explain how a bill becomes a law. They learn that a member of, say, the House of Representatives introduces a bill that is then referred to the relevant committee. The committee holds hearings at which interested parties testify. It then votes on amendments and whether to report the bill to the floor of the House. There, the bill is subject to further amendment and a vote on final passage. The same process takes place in the Senate. Differences are worked out between the two bodies in a conference committee. Finally, the bill goes to the president for signature or veto. How a bill becomes law is known by members of Congress as the "regular order." The problem is that there has been a breakdown of the regular order so that very few bills become law. As a result of the failure of Congress to exercise its legislative powers, the executive branch has become the chief source of federal decision making, circumventing the process so carefully designed in our Constitution.

The cause of the breakdown of the regular order is the oh-so-clever political tactic of putting the opposing party on the spot by forcing votes where members on the other side would take unpopular positions. Both parties have used the tactic, but in recent years it has grown from an occasional trick to the normal way Congress does business. In the first year of the Reagan presidency, Democratic senators offered a series of emotionally charged floor amendments to budget resolutions. The proposed amendments attacked the basic principle of Reaganomics, which was cutting both taxes and government spending. The proposed amendments paired programs for veterans, children, and the disabled with tax cuts for the rich and corporations, and made Republicans who supported the president seem callous about their most vulnerable constituents. Especially in my last term in the Senate, Republicans used the same tactic on Democrats. At our weekly luncheon of Republican senators, members would often rise with diabolical schemes to embarrass Democrats, usually adding with a smirk, "Make them vote on it." Jesse Helms of North Carolina was a master of concocting embarrassing amendments, especially to bills that funded the National Endowment for the Arts. His favorite target was the work of photographer Robert

Mapplethorpe, which, said Jesse, was obscene and blasphemous. He brought stacks of Mapplethorpe photos to the Senate floor to shock members. I must say that while I opposed the overly broad and politically contrived Helms amendments, the photos were not the sort I would hang on my living room wall.

In the years leading up to the 2014 election, then Senate majority leader Harry Reid understandably concluded that he would prefer to spare members of his party from voting on amendments that would be used against them in campaign advertising. He accomplished his aim by using his power to control the flow of action on the floor so that difficult amendments would not be in order. Bills did not reach the floor that he did not personally approve, and amendments could not be offered without his agreement. The result was that the normal process of the Senate was aborted, and the opportunity for senators to have a meaningful role in policymaking was nonexistent. Committees could hold hearings, but they did not adopt amendments or report bills of which the majority leader disapproved. The same applied for action on the floor. If a senator wanted to raise an issue he thought would improve a bill, that was too bad unless the majority leader consented.

The result of Senator Reid's strategy was that the Senate did very little. Budget resolutions often draw controversial amendments, so four years passed before Congress finally enacted a budget in late 2013. Think about it. The government taxed trillions of dollars and spent much more than that without the discipline of a budget to control what it was doing. Each year, Congress is supposed to pass twelve appropriations bills, each governing spending on specific areas such as the military, public works, and education, but fearing difficult votes on amendments, Congress took a less threatening course. It passed continuing resolutions, lumping what would be specific bills together in one package and adopting the spending decisions of earlier years. The continuing resolution strategy had two negative consequences. One was that while government's spending priorities change from year to year, appropriations did not change. For example, the military may decide that it needs a certain weapons system, but that doesn't mean that it needs the system every year at the expense of new priorities. Adopting continuing resolutions year after year allowed for no congressional flexibility in funding the evolving needs of government. The second was that combining all appropriations into a single resolution increased the threat of a government shutdown. It made it possible to defund not just part of government but all of government that requires appropriations.

Of course, Republicans shared the blame, perhaps most of it, for the stalemate in Washington. Their delight in offering legislation designed to cause political problems for Democrats was the majority leader's rationale for not allowing bills to reach the Senate floor. Then there was the filibuster, real or threatened, with the effect that nothing proceeded without the approval of a good number of Republicans, and if it did proceed, progress could take days. The result of Democratic fear of casting politically difficult votes and Republican delight in offering politically charged amendments and threatening the filibuster was summed up by a current member of the Senate who told me, "We don't do anything."

When there is little for them to do in Washington, members of Congress have plenty of time to be elsewhere, preparing for the next election so that if victorious they can continue to do little except to prepare themselves for the election after that. Some of this extra time is spent back home, attending events, keeping in touch with constituents, and, especially, tending to the base of supporters they most count on in their campaigns. For Republicans, this entails speaking at Lincoln Day dinners held on a statewide and countywide basis. For Democrats the comparable dinners are called Jefferson-Jackson Day.

But much more important to the candidate than the number of events attended is the number of dollars raised, and it is here where politicians without great wealth who cannot self-finance their campaigns are at a terrific disadvantage. In Missouri, for example, a campaign for the U.S. Senate costs in the neighborhood of $16 million to $20 million. As decided by the Supreme Court, outsiders, including political action committees, can spend unlimited amounts of money trying to influence the outcome of an election. A wealthy activist can produce advertising saying whatever he or she likes about candidates and issues. But candidates can receive no more than a statutorily fixed amount per donor per election.* This means that it is much more time-consuming for a candidate to raise the funds to define the message he or she wants to present than it is for well-heeled outsiders to do the defining. My view is that it is unfair to put a candidate at a disadvantage compared to outsiders. If outsiders can spend whatever they like to win an election, the candidate shouldn't be restricted to raising funds in limited increments. It would be better to remove or greatly increase limits on what a candidate's campaign can raise per contributor and concentrate instead on instantaneous reporting so the public can discover where the money is coming from.

To compete with large amounts of money that outsiders can pump into elections, candidates must devote huge amounts of time to raising funds in relatively small increments. Under congressional ethics rules, none of

* In 2016, individual contributors to Senate campaigns may give a maximum of $5,400 per election. A donor may contribute $2,700 to the primary campaign and another $2,700 for the general election.

this can be done from the office of a senator or congress-man. So when a senator is in Washington, he cannot pick up his office phone and call a prospective donor. Instead, he must leave his office and go to a private building to make his calls. The difference between picking up the phone on Capitol Hill and picking up the phone a few blocks away is quite seriously said to be the difference between what is ethical and what is not.

And most fund-raising isn't done as easily as making phone calls. Most fund-raising requires the candidate's physical presence at receptions or dinners. Some of these events are held in the candidate's district or state, but many are not. So most candidates in Senate elections travel far and wide in search of money. A senator from Missouri will certainly make several trips to New York and others to Chicago, Houston, Dallas, and so forth. The Senate schedule makes this possible. Typically, the Senate is in recess one in every four or five weeks and for a month or more in the summer. When it is in session, the normal workweek begins at 5:30 on Monday afternoons and ends at around 2:00 p.m. on Thursday. This leaves four days a week for campaign-related travel. In sum, Congress has devised a system where its members have little to do in Washington and much to do on the road.

The road show together with the high cost of living in Washington discourages families, especially those with school-age children, from moving to the capital to be with members who are likely to be somewhere else. Absent physical presence and families, there is little social interaction among members of Congress. This is a very significant change from the past. Former senator Howard Baker told me that when his parents served in Congress early in the twentieth century, travel between Tennessee and Washington being much more onerous than it is today, members would be full-time in Washington for about half the year and full-time at home the other half. This made it possible to have relatively normal lives in two places. Lawyers, for example, could practice in their home communities for about six months, truly identifying with the lives of their constituents, and they could spend six uninterrupted months in Washington in off- as well as on-the-job company with their colleagues.

The Senate's schedule was pretty much as it is now when I served in the Senate. Still, the desperate need to keep up in fund-raising with outside spenders was less acute then, so we could enjoy a more normal family and social life in Washington. Sally and I had a house in Washington, and our children attended area schools. Other than election years, when I spent nearly every available day campaigning in Missouri, I was in the state maybe five or six days a month, and I almost never visited other states for fund-raising. We were in Washington enough to get to know other senators and their families. We were in their homes, and they were in ours. Our closest friends were as likely to be Democrats as Republicans. In short, I knew the people with whom I worked not only as politicians I battled for or against in the Capitol but as human beings with real lives, and I liked them as human beings.

There's a lot of political appeal in telling constituents that you dislike Washington as much as many of them do, that you are not part of the inside-the-Beltway crowd, and that you enjoy nothing more than a good Fourth of July parade with home folks. I said much the same thing many times, and I believed it. I never thought of Washington as my home, but rather as my workstation. But it is important to know, really know, your colleagues, and it's difficult to know them if your only contact is as a political friend or foe.

Has politics changed in the last couple of decades? We know it has. It's become much meaner, much more polarized, and much more dysfunctional. Surely there are several reasons for this: talk radio, wedge issues, and others. I don't know of any scientific study to prove my point, but there is no doubt in my mind that the collapse of social interaction is a major cause of the breakdown of civility and cooperation in Washington. It is impossible to treat someone as an enemy if you have just had dinner in his home.

I can't understand why anyone would want to serve in Congress under the current state of affairs. The job itself seems pointless, as there is little to do legislatively. Even in the rare event that you might do something to affect public policy, your success could be quickly undone by executive order. You would know your colleagues as politicians, but not as friends. You would spend much of your time on the road, meaning that wherever you were, your family would be somewhere else. No wonder many people in Congress want to leave and many people we should hope would want to run for Congress refuse to do so. I do not think it is nostalgia for the past that leads me to observe that over the last twenty years there has been a dramatic decline in the quality of people in Congress.

Beyond wringing our hands, is there anything we can do, something creative, something that would improve the chaotic state of politics? I believe that the answer is yes, that it would be a form of ministry, and that it would be a gift of the faithful to America. It would be a religious ministry in two ways: It would bring order out of chaos, and it would help bind us together. Implementing the strategy would be risky, especially for members of Congress and people who run for Congress. It would call them to leave the safe confines of conventional thinking and the status quo. It would open them to opposition within their parties, ridicule by the punditry, and defeat in primary elections. But taking such risks is the way of religion.

An effective strategy would require participation both by politicians and by concerned citizens. What follows are some suggestions for how we might proceed. You may disagree with them and have ideas of your own. That's fine. But whatever your thoughts about specifics, let's think creatively about ordering chaos and bringing the country together.

A congressional contribution toward improving politics should begin with a systematic attempt to encourage greater collegiality among members of Congress. An easy place to start would be to arrange regular, hopefully weekly, opportunities for members to break bread together on a bipartisan basis. This would be a significant change from the current practice of Democrats and Republicans meeting in separate party caucuses each of the three weekdays when the Senate is in session. One possibility would be for members of each committee to meet periodically, not necessarily for the purpose of discussing legislation, but simply to get to know one another. For many years, the weekly Senate prayer breakfast has been the occasion for participating senators of both parties to gather in a friendly setting. That could be the model for additional and more widely attended common meals.

Another way to increase collegiality is to encourage travel by members of Congress. Traveling together is an excellent way of making friends. You are in each other's company for extended periods of time on airplanes, over meals, and at meetings. I did not know the then freshman senator from Montana, Max Baucus, until we went to Thailand and the border of Cambodia in 1979. The flight to Thailand consisted of three legs of about seven hours each, and along with Tennessee's Jim Sasser, we stayed at the U.S. ambassador's residence in Bangkok. By the end of the trip, we knew each other quite well. Sometime after our trip, I baptized Max's son, Zeno, at St. Alban's Church in Washington.

Max, a Democrat, and I, a Republican, were members of the Senate Finance Committee, where we worked closely together on international trade issues. We were deeply involved in what became the Trade Act of 1984 as well as the Senate's approval of the North American Free Trade Agreement ten years later. I have no doubt that our ability to work closely together across party lines was greatly enhanced by a friendship that began on our trip to Southeast Asia.

Much of what we saw on that trip was grim—refugees lying on the ground, dying of starvation. But in general, congressional travel is the opposite of grim. Congressional delegations, known as Codels, depart from Andrews Air Force Base, just over the District of Columbia line in Maryland. The planes are similar to those flown by commercial airlines, but painted blue and white with the words "United States of America." The cabins are spaciously configured for comfortable long-distance travel. Trips are staffed by military officers, typically Air Force majors or colonels and sergeants who handle logistical

needs such as luggage. Codel destinations can be anywhere in the world. Many trips are to troubled places
such as Iraq and Afghanistan. Others are to Europe and
other pleasant locales. As chair of the Senate's International Trade Subcommittee, I led delegations to China,
Japan, and South Korea. I also traveled to Geneva for
trade negotiations and to Brussels and Moscow in connection with an arms treaty with the then Soviet Union.

Such travel is the object of criticism in the media as
well as by opponents in reelection campaigns. Critics dis-
miss Codels as junkets and a waste of taxpayers' money.
In my view, these trips are very important for two reasons.
First, and most obviously, they greatly deepen a participant's knowledge of subjects before Congress. I could
not have been an effective participant in U.S. trade policy without being present at trade negotiations and being
familiar with the policymakers of other countries. Second, and I think even more important, travel is an opportunity to spend time with colleagues and get to know
them as persons. Yes, there is a budgetary cost to congressional travel, but it is such a minuscule part of government's spending that focusing on it amounts to straining
at gnats. Travel is a practical way, and unfortunately one
of the few ways, of bringing a polarized Congress at least
somewhat closer together. Travel is worth the price, and
we should encourage it.

An important way to encourage collegiality would be

to make it more attractive for congressional families to move to Washington. This would increase opportunities for members to interact in social rather than strictly professional levels.

Congress should consider a financial package that encourages families to stay together. The package could include moving expenses, a housing allowance, tuition support, and an increase in congressional pay. Each such proposal is certain to draw heated protests as well as election problems, as nothing is more likely to evoke the anger of citizens than proposals to increase congressional pay. On an afternoon radio broadcast in St. Louis, the late Bob Hardy announced that the Senate was about to vote on a pay raise. Within hours, my office received 170 phone calls, all of which were strongly opposed to the idea. Campaign commercials are frequently to the effect that "Congressman Jones voted to raise his own pay twenty-three times." On the other hand, conservative supporters of family values might show some interest in an effort to improve family life in Congress. Perhaps an independent commission could make recommendations on the status of congressional families.

Moving families to Washington would increase collegiality only if members would be there as well. To keep them in town would require reorganizing congressional schedules and reforming campaign finance laws in a way contrary to conventional wisdom. The three-day workweek should be expanded to five with the assurance of free evenings so members can socialize. Congress should make it easier for candidates to raise campaign funds by removing or greatly increasing the limits on contributions individuals can make to a candidate's own committee, thereby creating a level playing field for candidates who must compete against independent individuals and PACs. The automatic response of supporters of campaign finance reform would be vehement opposition to any proposal that would relax limits on political fund-raising. However, the Supreme Court has ruled out limits on outsiders, and it does not serve the cause of good government for candidates to be at a disadvantage in defining their own message. In addition, it would serve the cause of good government if members of Congress spent less time on the road raising money and more time interacting with their colleagues.

Improving collegiality should be the goal of Congress as a whole. Beyond that, committed members could organize themselves to develop tactics to make government work.

Congress is replete with what its members call caucuses, that is, groups of members who join together to advance common concerns. The Congressional Black Caucus is the best known of these groupings, but there are many others. My colleague from Missouri, Kit Bond, chaired the

Senate's National Guard Caucus, which, as its name indicates, champions the cause of the National Guard. Suppose there were a Make Government Work Caucus, a group of senators (and another of representatives) who devise and execute strategies for the purpose of making government work. Made up of both Democrats and Republicans, the caucus would not be in business to serve the interests of either party or to advance a liberal or conservative ideology. It would exist for the single purpose of repairing what is now broken, government, and its starting point would be fixing Congress. How might such a caucus work?

First, members of the caucus could vote as a bloc to table, that is to set aside, mischievous floor amendments offered solely for the purpose of embarrassing the other party. Members would vote aye on motions to table whether they happened to agree or disagree with the substance of the proposed amendment. Their vote would be cast for the one purpose of moving the business of government forward. Setting aside pernicious amendments would obviate the reason Harry Reid gave for keeping legislation off the floor.

I used tabling motions to set aside amendments Jesse Helms offered on bills to fund the National Endowment for the Arts. In the Senate, a motion to table is not debatable, and calls for an immediate vote, so my motions had the effect of pulling the plug on Jesse's tactic. Of course, it infuriates members of your own party to block what they consider a very clever political move. I have a vivid memory of Jesse Helms stalking off the Senate floor after I had succeeded in tabling one of his amendments, snarling at me, "Thanks a bunch." It is a very uncomfortable feeling when a senator makes members of his party angry, and members of a Make Government Work Caucus should be prepared to be uncomfortable. But I think it would be easier for them if they were to stake out their strategy in advance and apply it on a consistent basis.

A second strategy of a Make Government Work Caucus would be to vote to invoke cloture on all matters not involving significant issues of public policy only after members of the minority party have had a reasonable opportunity to offer amendments. Majority Leader Reid routinely and unfairly filed cloture petitions immediately on calling up a bill, thereby severely limiting the right of the minority to introduce and debate amendments. A Make Government Work Caucus would give the minority a fair chance to offer amendments before voting for cloture. Today the filibuster and threats of filibuster have become commonplace, as has been the routine use of cloture. If a bipartisan group of senators would band together and vote for or against cloture in order to make the Senate work, the filibuster and cloture would be far less effective in blocking Senate action.

Again, those members of the minority party who delight in halting the Senate's work would be angered by their colleagues who vote for cloture. But if the strategy is announced in advance, and if it is followed consistently, the obstructionists would have fair warning, and the strategy of the caucus, if not admired, would at least be understandable.

A third strategy of a Make Government Work Caucus would be to support some selected legislative initiatives where the caucus could reach agreement on areas of public policy. This would differ from the procedural strategies of tabling pernicious amendments and voting for or against cloture to end filibusters, strategies that would require no agreement on the underlying issue. Merely removing congressional obstruction is such a worthy goal that I would not allow differences on any substantive matter to interrupt the work of the caucus. Still, if a bipartisan group could fashion an agreement on almost any legislation, that would be strong evidence that government can be made to function.

The so-called Gang of Eight senators who in 2013 worked together to propose immigration reform legislation is a good model for how the caucus might proceed. Four members of the Gang of Eight were Democrats and four were Republicans, and they all were able to reach agreement on very controversial proposals. Over the years, many politicians have said that addressing our government's budget crisis would require compromises that seem politically suicidal, with Democrats agreeing to restrain entitlement spending and Republicans agreeing to raise taxes. So the saying goes that the two parties should "hold hands and jump over the cliff together." But the parties do not hold hands, and they balk at the sight of the cliff. So the national debt grows dramatically with no serious effort to curtail it.

The key to success of any caucus approach to legislation is that the members act together as a bloc and not as a loose collection of individuals, each of whom is prepared to act separately. This means that they would have to work out whatever differences they have among themselves and, after they reach their own agreement, go forth as a unit. That is a tall order, because members of Congress are reluctant to give up their independence. Other members of Congress and representatives of the administration would attempt to dislodge each participant with offers of side deals that might be quite appealing to members of the caucus. However, as the old adage goes, "The perfect is the enemy of the good." The temptation to go independently for the perfect can undermine the effort the group makes to achieve the good.

Here's an example of how a caucus might work, although it isn't squarely on point because all the senators in the group were Republicans. In 1991, a group of nine Republican senators undertook the challenge of passing civil rights legislation where Senator Kennedy had failed the year before. Negotiations with the administration were contentious, and the administration would have liked to pick off members, but we held together, subordinating what might have been individual preferences to what we had agreed on as a group. We succeeded in passing a bill that President George H. W. Bush signed in a Rose Garden ceremony. Ted Kennedy, too, refused to let his view of the perfect undermine the good he could accomplish with our cooperation. After reaching agreement with our group of Republicans he managed the bill on the floor of the Senate and moved to table amendments offered by liberal Democrats, even though those amendments were more to his liking than what we had written in the bill. The key is that no disagreements on specific legislation be permitted to divert the caucus from its objective of making government work.

In 2013, while meeting with a bipartisan group of chiefs of staff of senators, each of whom expressed dismay at the inability of the Senate to do anything, I proposed the same idea I have suggested here of a group of senators banding together to draft and pass some piece of legislation. The chief of staff of a western Democrat promptly said that the idea wouldn't work, because the Senate leadership would "punish" those who participated. When I asked what he meant by punish, he said that the leader, Harry Reid, would retaliate by shutting the offending senator off from advancing legislation and introducing floor amendments. My own thought is that it isn't much of a punishment to prevent a member from doing something in a Senate that doesn't do anything. But I am not there, and I suppose that for someone who wants to be in Congress it's difficult to forgo even such crumbs as the majority leader lets fall from his table. Members of Congress want to have a somewhat meaningful job, so an initiative contrary to the wishes of the leadership is risky.

To have a chance of success, members of a Make Government Work Caucus would need to be bold. It would not be pleasant to be on the wrong side of the leadership by joining a bipartisan attempt to legislate. When pushed, members of the caucus would have to push back in a very public way. They should tell the public what it already knows—that government is broken—and they should explain that their strategy is an effort to fix it. If the leader punishes them, they should make as much noise as possible. They should tell the public just what is happening and why. If they stand their ground, they will be respected for doing so. I don't think that standing firm in an effort to fix government is a suicide mission. I believe it would work if executed boldly.

I think that, but I'm not certain. Members of a Make Government Work Caucus would face the wrath not only of colleagues but of constituents who don't want compromise, don't want bipartisan cooperation, don't want government to work. And such anger would mean more than noisy confrontations at town hall meetings. It would mean likely opposition in the next primary election and possible defeat. That is precisely why those who would undertake it would be performing a religious act.

For me or anyone else in private life to suggest that members of Congress pursue a collegiality agenda and form a Make Government Work Caucus is a bit like asking a soldier to charge an enemy's gun emplacement. It is easy to ask someone else to take a risk when we occupy comfortable positions of safety. But what can we as ordinary citizens, who don't have to face elections, do to help bring order out of the present state of political chaos? It is clear that if any effort to reform politics is to succeed, we must be more than innocent bystanders. For starters, we should understand that reform-minded politicians will not last long enough to accomplish their objectives without the strong support of citizens who help them win elections and withstand the blowback they will certainly face once in office. This will take terrific effort, because strong counterforces will be at work. As noted, congressional leaders will want to punish members who push independent legislative initiatives. Partisan firebrands would likely gin up primary opponents for senators who vote for tabling motions and cloture resolutions. Back home, party activists would try to defeat incumbents who worked with the other side to end Washington's gridlock.

Talk radio hosts would be apoplectic. What's more, opposition would come from across the spectrum and would include good-government types who would strongly oppose looser restraints on fund-raising and new incentives for families to move to Washington. Against such a force, the counterpush would have to be Herculean.

That means that supporters of reform would have to be vocal and well organized. They would have to attend town hall meetings and be at least as outspoken as their vociferous opponents. They would have to make their presence known in social media, by letters to the editor, and by call-ins to radio shows. They would have to form alternative organizations to counter the opposition. Finally, they would have to be realistic about the importance of money in political campaigns and do what does not come naturally for reform-minded citizens. They would have to raise large sums of money to support candidates who work for change. They should form good-government political action committees. In sum, I am suggesting that people who want to make government work must become activists. People who want to mend American politics must become even more engaged and more effective than those who have broken it.

How can we think that such a practical approach to political organizing is religious? Consider the charge Jesus gave when he sent his disciples into the towns and villages. They were to proclaim the kingdom, cure the sick, and raise the dead—all good works. But they were not to be pushovers. "If anyone will not welcome you or listen to your words, shake off the dust from your feet." Then Jesus added, "See, I am sending you out like sheep in the midst of wolves; so be wise as serpents and innocent as doves" (Matthew 10:5–16). The disciples were not huddled in a cloister, they were sent into the rough-and-tumble world of wolves. If that were so for followers of Jesus who were to proclaim the kingdom of God, it is equally true for citizens who would reform politics.

Election campaigns are in obvious need of reform, but since the Supreme Court has foreclosed curtailing their financing, we should consider other possibilities. A good place to start would be to underscore what everyone knows, but too easily accepts. Today's political campaigns are miserable affairs, devoid of substance and replete with smear, and they warrant our vocal condemnation. They are so vacuous as to be unworthy of even the passing attention of voters, their messages come in short, venomous bursts through thirty-second commercials and robo-calls, and they are reported by a media fixated on polls and tactics and bored by the direction of the country.

Debates between candidates are the most ballyhooed and allegedly informative events of most campaigns, but their format makes them next to useless. The usual model is the way presidential debates were conducted before

1996: a panel of reporters, each vying to steal the show with clever questions candidates had no idea were coming. The typical ninety-minute debates were divided into five-minute segments in which each candidate was given two minutes to answer and thirty seconds to respond. So, for example, a candidate might have been asked to explain his position on the Middle East in a total of two and a half minutes. Often the subjects covered have not been nearly as significant as the Middle East, and were sometimes "off the wall." Spontaneity and quickness afoot have been the prime values emphasized in most debates, rather than thoughtful discussion of public issues.

The disconnect between political debates and reality is that spontaneity is seldom a required or even a desirable quality in an officeholder. Policy issues call for thoughtfulness, not quickness. Of interest to voters is where the candidate would lead us, not whether he or she can come up with an off-the-top-of-the-head response in a "lightning round" of questions. In the early presidential debates, candidates seemed more concerned about avoiding embarrassing mistakes than elucidating consequential positions. Debate preparation resembled cramming for exams for fear that a panelist would ask a question the responder had never considered. Some past questions have been surprises to candidates and of no possible use in educating voters. Questions to presidential candidates have included what portraits they would hang in the Cabinet Room and whether they preferred Coke or Pepsi, the latter by John King in a so-called lightning round for Republican hopefuls in 2012. Gubernatorial candidates in Massachusetts were asked to tell voters when was the last time they cried.

The standard tactic for challengers is to demand a series of debates "just like Lincoln-Douglas." But there is nothing about modern debates that remotely resembles Lincoln-Douglas. Then, the two great contenders for the Senate squared off in seven debates of three hours each on the nation-defining issue of slavery. No panelists from the media butted in with cute questions about the candidates' preferences for soft drinks.

In 1996, the Commission on Presidential Debates, on which I serve, moved from a panel of media to a single moderator. More dramatically, in 2012 the format changed to fifteen-minute segments on subjects announced in advance. These have been positive changes, although my own preference would be for much longer segments and a moderator who ensured a fair distribution of time, but otherwise got out of the way.

As for television and radio commercials, they are almost exclusively negative. The typical message is on the order of "Vote for me, because my opponent is self-serving and possibly corrupt, and he enjoys hurting people like you." There is almost nothing said about the candidate's own qualifications or how he or she would govern if elected. Of course, campaigns have long been a nasty business, notably the presidential election of 1884 in which his opponents accused Grover Cleveland, a bachelor, of fathering a son. The difference today is that with the predominance of the thirty-second commercial and social media, campaigns offer nothing in addition to the nasty. They amount to pure venom unadulterated by substance. Their aim isn't to enhance the image of a candidate but to drive up the negatives of the opponent, with the result that it is now common for both major-party candidates to have higher negative ratings than positive. Every two years, most of us, quite predictably, claim that we detest all this negative campaigning, saying so in self-righteous terms. Then two years later the same thing happens, only more so, for the simple reason that it works; it wins elections. We announce that we hate it with our words, and we reward it with our votes.

The widely suspected consequence of the miserable state of campaigns is that good people stay away from politics, especially those who might otherwise consider running for office. While I don't know how to prove this suspicion, it surely must be true. But whether or not this is the case, there are other, even more important reasons why the present state of campaigns does great injury to America. First, it undermines the foundation of who we are, our republican form of government. That is, vacuous campaigns deprive citizens of their right to set the course for our country when they choose their elected representatives. Yes, they can go to the polls and vote for this candidate or that, but when a campaign is no more than sound bites, pseudo-debates, and dire warnings that the opponent is a crook, there is little basis for electing someone who represents their informed opinions. Representative democracy backfires. Second, campaigns of half-minute commercials and sound-bite-length debate responses direct our attention away from the big questions toward short, opportunistic answers, and thereby prevent us from weighing alternative policies that would affect the future of the country. For example, campaigns transform broad questions of economic policy into a list of unpopular specifics with which to attack opponents. That was the fate of the balanced and highly regarded report of the Simpson-Bowles Commission that made a number of recommendations that, if taken together, would create a sustainable federal budget. But when broken into sound-bite-size pieces, Simpson-Bowles became an assortment of campaign commercials that attacked its supporters for wanting to reduce the home mortgage deduction, increase the gas tax, and raise the Social Security retirement age. It might be possible for the American people to agree with a compromise package of proposals that would strengthen the country, but it's smart politics to break the package into its unpopular parts and use those parts in thirty-second attacks.[*]

The present state of political campaigns should be of such particular concern to faithful people as to impel us to be active reformers. Many Americans profess distaste for politics, but the faithful should find it worse than distasteful. It is in opposition to what we believe and to who we should be, so we have a religious obligation to change it.

Because God calls us to be cocreators, advancing the kingdom on earth, we should demand a political framework that enables us to answer that call. The present framework does the opposite. It excludes the possibility of our informed participation in decision making, miniaturizing major issues into one-liners and reducing directional choices to personal attacks. If given the opportunity to reflect on the course our communities and our country should take, we will draw different conclusions about platforms and candidates. Faithful people will span the spectrum of liberal and conservative, but wherever we are on the spectrum, we will be doing our best to make our communities and our country better. That is God's work. By denying us meaningful participation in deciding our future, the present state of politics turns us from that work.

[*] Brian Faler, "The Ghost of Simpson-Bowles Haunts 2014," *Politico,* October 25, 2014.

Thirty-second commercials, robo-calls, short answers to big questions, and the social media are powerful tools for the work politicians do so well, pandering to our self-interest. The utility of these tools was demonstrated in attacks on supporters of Simpson-Bowles. It takes but a few seconds to assert that we will lose our benefits. It takes time to make the case for the common good, that without a change of course future generations will inherit bankrupt programs and a bankrupt country. Our early presidents emphasized the critical importance of virtue. Religion pulls us toward virtue, but modern campaign techniques move us ever further away from the common good and ever closer to concern for self and little else. If faithful people intend to be a more effective force in directing America toward virtue, our agenda should include creating new tools of our own to counter the tools of politics.

The most useful tools that the faithful should use are not really new, but a rediscovery of something old. Think Lincoln-Douglas and three-hour debates on one issue. Think *The Federalist Papers* and lengthy exposition of the intent and design of our government. In sum, we should create new ways of enriching political discourse. We would not be able to put an end to the thirty-second commercial or the twenty-second sound bite. We would not succeed in dissuading the media from covering election-year "horse races" at the expense of substance, but we could at least supplement the perverse frivolity that is the essence of modern elections and crowds out everything of value.

For starters, faithful people should make our voices heard, loudly calling candidates and the media to task for their disservice to the country. More constructively, we should create new forums for discussing public issues in a much more extensive and informative way than we find in today's campaigns. For example, a congregation or, even better, a cluster of congregations might sponsor an evening program on a single subject such as the future of Social Security or America's role in the Middle East. Other forums might be of more local interest such as schools and transportation. The goal would be to enrich the tone and content of civic discussion, not to turn congregations into advocacy groups for specific policies. For each forum a knowledgeable person would serve as a resource to provide background information. Invitations to participate would go to officeholders and candidates. The keys would be to stay on one subject for a sufficient length of time to cover important points and foster an atmosphere of civility. Would politicians attend such an event? Many would rather not, as they would prefer ducking big issues to discussing them. But if the audience were large and the evening were well publicized, they would feel compelled to attend.

Creative people will come up with better ideas than I

have for enriching public discourse, and implementing any idea would take hard work and perseverance. It would be worth the effort, because it would be a very real contribution to our country by elevating the level of policymaking. And by calling citizens to look beyond themselves to consideration of the common good, it would be a practical response to the call of our faith.

In addition to enriching the content of political discourse, faithful people could play active parts in changing its tone. The relentless personal attacks that are the heart of nearly every campaign sharply contrast with the Sermon on the Mount, where Jesus said that anyone who calls a brother or sister a fool "will be liable to the hell of fire" (Matthew 5:22). Then Jesus added that we should do more than merely refrain from making insults, we should love our enemies and pray for those who persecute us (Matthew 5:44). Paul taught that we should "bless those who persecute you" and "if your enemies are hungry, feed them" (Romans 12:14, 12:20). He said we should pray for "kings and all who are in high positions" (Timothy 2:1–2).

These repeated New Testament admonitions on how Christians are supposed to treat others warrant three observations. First, the enemies and rulers of whom the Bible speaks are far different from the sort of political adversaries we know in the United States. However they might disagree with each other, Democrats and Republicans are not enemies. They don't persecute each other. When Paul urged Christians to pray for all who were in high positions, he was requesting prayers for rulers who targeted followers of Jesus for corporal punishment and death. If Christians can find it in them to pray for rulers who kill them, all the more ready we should be to pray for presidents or members of Congress with whom we merely disagree on questions of policy.

Second, neither Jesus nor Paul asked us to pray that those who oppose us change their minds. They did not suggest prayers that persecutors stop being persecutors or that enemies become agreeable. There was no expectation of reciprocal kindness. Instead, we are to bless our persecutors while they are persecuting us. We are to feed our enemies while they are our enemies. In the church I attend, we pray for the president of the United States. I include the president in my personal prayers. This does not mean that I support the president politically or pray that he will see the light and come to agree with my opinions. We pray for the president simply because he is the president. We pray for politicians while we do our best to defeat them. Just as there is no inconsistency between praying for and being in opposition to the "enemies" of New Testament times, there is no inconsistency today between praying for and trying to defeat those on the opposite side of political controversies.

Third, there is a big difference between opposition and abuse. We can strongly oppose someone in politics and still treat our opponent with dignity. A consequence of prayer is that it facilitates respectful opposition. It's difficult to be simultaneously prayerful and abusive toward opponents. Religious people have a responsibility for treating their adversaries prayerfully and respectfully. By doing so, they would help create a new tone for American politics.

An agenda for citizens takes more than acknowledging that the tone of political campaigns violates the clear mandates of religion; it needs a tactic that faithful people put into action. So here's an idea. Suppose we make it our business to get in the faces of candidates with this direct question: "Please explain how the commercial that you just ran and I just saw squares with your values." If the candidate is running for Congress or president, the question would ask for an explanation of "the commercial you said you approved." The tagline "I approve this message" was a requirement added to the law by the McCain-Feingold Act of 2002 on the theory that if a candidate took personal responsibility for a commercial, the content would be more measured than if the sponsor were an anonymous "committee." If the requirement ever served its intended purpose, it clearly does not do so now. Candidates appear to have no shame in approving the most scurrilous of attacks. So let's up the ante. Let's ask candidates to move beyond an acknowledgment to explanations of how their campaigns reflect their values. We should ask the question at places and times where we can put candidates on the spot, hopefully when TV cameras are present. And if a candidate denies that a commercial is true to his or her character, we should ask that it be taken off the air.

Beyond reforming the content and style of campaigns, members of the public can help politicians be in practice what they are at their core—authentically human. Particularly, we can help them recover what most politicians have lost: a sense of humor.

Exhibit A of what politicians have lost is the very funny YouTube video of juggler/comedian Michael Davis at Ford's Theatre on September 25, 1982.* That was a high-pressure time in politics, just after President Reagan had scored major victories over House Speaker Tip O'Neill on spending and tax cuts and just before the Democrats won their own victories in the 1982 off-year election. The video shows the president and the Speaker along with Howard and Joy Baker roaring with laughter in the front row as they watch the comedian juggle an apple, an egg, and a bowling ball. As you are watching this on YouTube,

---

* "Michael Davis Ford's Theater part 2 (Ronald Reagan & Tip O'Neil [sic] laughing together hysterically)," YouTube, http://www.youtube.com/watch?v=n6mbW-jMtrY.

which I recommend not just for the fun of it but for a purpose, ask yourself these questions: Can you imagine this happening today? Can you imagine the president, the Speaker of the House, and the majority leader of the Senate out together for a fun evening? Can you imagine them laughing? And if you can't imagine such a thing today, what do you think is missing in politics? In my mind, what's missing is more than a sense of humor. Some people are funnier and some laugh more readily than others. But uproarious laughter at Ford's Theatre is a group enterprise. It happens when people are together and at ease. This is why laughter is contagious. When we are alone, we may see something funny and chuckle quietly, but to rock our heads back and forth and roar is social.

I witnessed the Reagan-O'Neill relationship when I was seated with them at a White House luncheon marking the hundredth anniversary of Harry Truman's birth. I have no recollection of what they said, but I clearly recall the laughter and their obvious enjoyment of each other's company. I think their personal relationship helped them get on with the business of government regardless of their sharp differences.

Ronald Reagan was a master of self-effacing humor, which in debating Walter Mondale he used to defuse concerns about his age. "I will not make age an issue in this campaign. I am not going to exploit, for political purposes, my opponent's youth and inexperience." To questions about whether he spent long enough hours at his job or took afternoon naps, he answered, "It's true hard work never killed anybody, but I figure, why take the chance?" On another occasion he said, "I have left orders to be awakened at any time in case of national emergency, even if I'm in a cabinet meeting."

Of course, there is a huge difference between laughing at one's self or good-natured kidding and cutting sarcasm that makes fun of others. We should be quick to condemn whatever belittles another person. But the best humor, the self-deprecating sort, is important in politics both as a social lubricant and as a reminder of the humanity of politicians. People who can laugh at themselves are not apt to be self-righteously fierce. Joy is the natural product of faith. In the words of Jesus, "I have said these things to you so that my joy may be in you, and that your joy may be complete" (John 15:11). We sing, "Joyful, Joyful We Adore Thee" and "Joy to the World." C. S. Lewis entitled the memoir of his early religious experience *Surprised by Joy.* Joy in God's love is the counterbalance of self-love, of the pompous assurance that we possess the last word. When we know the joy of God's love, we see everything else for what it is. We can laugh at ourselves, and when we do that we can more fully love our neighbors.

The decline of social interaction in Congress might

explain the demise of good-natured humor; so might the self-importance of officials who see nothing amusing in their work. But the explanation I hear repeatedly from people in or close to Congress boils down to a single word: fear. Politicians are afraid that if they try to be funny, it would backfire on them, and it probably would. Imagine what would happen to a president today who, like Reagan, joked that he should be awakened in cabinet meetings. It would be taken as an admission of inattention to duty. It would go viral on social media. It would consume segments on TV news channels. It would appear in campaign commercials. One member of the Senate told me that his colleagues are guarded even in conversations among themselves for fear that what they say may be recorded by an iPhone or similar device. The example some cite for the necessity of caution is the plight of former senator Trent Lott of Mississippi.

In December 2002, Lott, the Republican leader in the Senate, who was presumed to become majority leader the following month, made what he intended as a light-hearted comment at Strom Thurmond's hundredth birthday party: "I want to say this about my state: When Strom Thurmond ran for president, we voted for him. We're proud of it. And if the rest of the country had followed our lead, we wouldn't have had all these problems over all these years, either."

The media promptly jumped on the remark, turning

it into a major network news story. On *Hardball,* Chris Matthews claimed that many Republicans are "Dixiecrats to the heart of it." In the midst of the firestorm, Lott heeded numerous calls for his resignation as Republican leader and abandoned his certain January election as majority leader. To put Lott's remarks in context, Strom Thurmond had long since abandoned the segregationist policies he had espoused fifty-four years earlier as the Dixiecrat candidate for president, and by the time of his hundredth birthday had become a universally beloved personage in the Senate. It seemed that everyone had a favorite Strom Thurmond story to tell, and no one would have thought of him as a racist. Simply stated, Strom was a character. There is no possibility that in speaking at the birthday celebration, Trent Lott intended to endorse the Dixiecrat policies of 1948. Yet his lame attempt at humor became a turning point in his career and an unforgettable warning to politicians: If you're thinking about being funny, be very, very careful in what you say.

In the 2014 Iowa Senate campaign, incumbent Democratic senator Tom Harkin made this comment about Republican nominee Joni Ernst:

In this Senate race, I've been watching some of these ads. And there's sort of this sense that, "Well, I hear so much about Joni Ernst. She is really attractive, and she sounds nice." Well, I got to thinking about that. I don't care if she's as good-looking as Taylor Swift or as nice as Mr. Rogers, but if she votes like Michele Bachmann, she's wrong for the state of Iowa.

Ernst promptly responded, "I am offended, . . . if my name were John Ernst and I were a guy he wouldn't be saying those things about me."

This incident warrants a couple of observations. The first is that there is no possibility that Tom Harkin, a liberal Democrat with whom I served, intended to give offense to anyone, and certainly not to women. The second is that it stretches the imagination to believe that Joni Ernst, a combat veteran whose campaign commercials claimed that she grew up on a farm castrating pigs, was truly offended by Harkin's remarks. But taking offense is a common tactic in politics. Harkin's comment was a weak attempt to be humorous that created a national uproar.

We have lost something important to both politics and religion when politicians cannot be themselves, when they must constantly be on guard lest they destroy their careers, when they eliminate from their jobs any sense of what should be joyful and at times ridiculous. That, I believe, is where we are today, so an agenda item for faithful citizens should be to accept the humanity of politicians who make what are obviously innocent mistakes.

All of us can advance this agenda item by simply being more tolerant of well-intentioned mishaps. We can see weak attempts at humor for what they are and not as malicious assaults on decency. We can call out politicians who feign offense and pundits who pounce at every opportunity, telling them in effect to get a life. That would be a good, informal approach we could take when occasions arise, and it would encourage politicians to be themselves. To that general awareness and response, I would add something more structured and more fun. This idea has as its model the "Pinocchios" awarded by the fact checker of *The Washington Post.* In the *Post* a minor political fib gets one Pinocchio; a whopper gets four.

Since a prize for lying is named after the fictitious Pinocchio, I propose that a prize for taking offense at humor be named after that fictitious and perpetually offended political buffoon of the Fred Allen radio show, Senator Beauregard Claghorn. Senator Claghorn's often repeated line was "It's a joke, son!" My idea is that we give a politician who claims offense, or a pundit who professes alarm at an innocent joke, one Claghorn. The deeper the offense taken, the more Claghorns awarded. Who would confer the award? All of us should. All of us should become members of the Beauregard Claghorn Society.

CHAPTER SIX

COMPROMISE AND PRINCIPLE

On August 11, 2011, at a time when bipartisan members of Congress were trying to work out an agreement on the federal budget, eight Republican presidential aspirants stood on an Iowa stage and dismissed any idea of compromise. When a media panelist asked whether there was any ratio of spending cuts to tax increases the candidates would accept, former senator Rick Santorum was the first to answer: "No. The answer is no." The debate's moderator, Bret Baier, then put all candidates on the spot. He posed the hypothetical of a budget agreement of ten dollars of "real spending cuts" for each dollar of tax increases and asked, "Can you raise your hand if you feel so strongly about not raising taxes, you'd walk away on a ten-to-one deal?" The Republican audience cheered as all eight candidates raised their hands. In the minds of eight would-be presidents and their partisans, the most serious issue before our country, controlling the national debt, was not a subject for negotiation. Because there is no possibility that Congress would agree to deficit reduction without at least some new taxes, the effect of walking away from a ten-to-one deal would be no agreement, and no effort to contain our growing debt.

The reason candidates took such an uncompromising position is clear. Any flexibility on tax increases would have alienated the Republican base, those voters who would attend party caucuses and perhaps decide the presidential nomination. A Pew Research Center Survey conducted in early 2014 found that the percentage of "consistently conservative" respondents who always vote in primary elections exceeded the percentage of "mostly conservative" voters by a margin of 54 percent to 32 percent. The comparable numbers for "consistently liberal" and "mostly liberal" respondents were 34 percent over 19 percent. On the question of whether respondents had contacted an elected official in the past two years, the consistently conservative exceeded the mostly conservative by 50 percent to 34 percent. The margin for liberals was 45 percent to 22 percent.[*]

Obviously, the most politically active people have the most influence. Citizens who vote decide elections, while those who stay home are powerless. Activists who call congressional offices and attend town hall meetings have more impact than people who do no more than go to the

[*] *Wall Street Journal,* June 20, 2014, A6.

polls. Responding to intensity, the natural approach of politicians is the same as that of people in business: tell customers, or voters, what they want to hear. Often when we complain about politics it's as though we are speaking of some strange and disengaged group of officeholders who have no relation to the real world in which we normal citizens live. But in fact, politicians are very engaged. They are most responsive to people who are in front of them, those who make the effort to call the office or attend the meeting. And people who put themselves in front of politicians are those with strong opinions, those most inclined to pull politics toward its polar extremes. The greater political participation of the ideologically committed has affected the makeup of Congress. According to one report, "Today, the most conservative Democrat in the House of Representatives or the Senate is to the left of the most liberal Republican."* The result is that when many people go to the polls for general elections, they would rather pull a lever for "none of the above" than the names chosen by political activists. This is precisely why it is important for a greater representation of concerned citizens to make its presence known well before general elections, and especially in primaries.

Since George H. W. Bush's famous line, "Read my

* *Governing in a Polarized America: A Bipartisan Blueprint to Strengthen Our Democracy,* Bipartisan Policy Center, Commission on Political Reform, 2014, 20.

lips. No new taxes," many Republicans have made opposition to tax increases an absolute principle. Grover Norquist's Americans for Tax Reform has persuaded nearly all Republican presidential and congressional candidates to sign pledges that they would vote against all proposals to raise tax rates or to reduce deductions and credits without matching rate cuts. Incumbents who support new taxes as part of a budget deal are certain to draw Tea Party opposition in primary elections, and support for such a deal cost President Bush reelection in 1992.

Nearly all Republicans agree on limiting taxes, but there is a significant difference between holding a political position and elevating it to the status of nonnegotiable principle. Transforming political positions into absolute principles makes government unworkable, as it is today. Some hard-core Republicans think that rigid adherence to a nonnegotiable position is consistent with conservatism. It is not. Let's first consider the practical necessity of compromise and then examine why turning debatable questions into absolute principles is not conservative.

Achieving compromise characterized the Senate tenure of Bob Dole, whose office as leader was, as it remains, on the second floor of the Capitol, a few steps away from the Senate floor. It consists of a couple of large, comfortable spaces sandwiching a cramped room with a single window. Most of that room is taken up by a conference table surrounded by chairs, with just enough space on the perimeter for staffers to stand. When Bob was our leader, his tactic for advancing difficult legislation was to ask any senator who had an interest to go to his office, which meant that room. Of course, we couldn't decline the invitation if we wanted to have input into a bill's progress. The result was a large number of senators huddled around a table, each accompanied by at least one staffer. The staffers, always holding sheaves of papers, positioned themselves along the walls like diagonally parked cars. I'm sure there must have been a ventilation system in the leader's office, but its effects were not noticeable. Negotiations could last for hours, and the atmosphere became progressively unbearable. To say the least, there was a strong incentive to bring the meetings to a conclusion.

I don't recall Bob Dole subjecting himself to many turns in his hot box. I do remember numerous occasions when I left the room desperate for a breath of air, and wandered into the Republican Cloakroom to find Bob sitting comfortably in a large leather chair, always with the same question: "Got it worked out yet?"

Whatever the antecedent of "it" on any given day, Bob wasn't asking what we were discussing or whether legislative ideas were to his liking. He was the leader of what has been called "the world's greatest deliberative body," and his aim was to make us deliberate, like it or not. And under his leadership the process did move forward. The results were seldom perfect by anyone's reckoning, but perfection wasn't the goal. To "work it out" was to reach a result that, for all its imperfections, was at least tolerable to enough legislators for it to become law.

Bob Dole understood that legislating requires negotiation and compromise. That is why he herded us into that unbearable hot box, and that is how he operated when he was chair of the Senate Finance Committee, the committee responsible for writing our tax laws. Tax legislation is complex and always unpopular with someone. If it relieves the tax burden somewhere, it increases the burden somewhere else. It may be "revenue neutral," that is, its intended effect may be no net change in the amount of revenue government raises, but tax legislation is not neutral toward everyone, and some people will always claim that, for them at least, it is a new tax. Bob Dole could not have agreed with the eight candidates on that stage in Iowa, because he knew how the legislative process worked, and he knew the importance of compromise.

Today, the legislative process does not work, because members of Congress do not work things out. And as the partisan audience in Iowa demonstrated by their cheering, their supporters don't want them to work things out. There's no way of knowing whether all of the eight who raised their hands in Iowa actually believed that a ten-for-one budget deal would be bad policy, or whether they were simply playing to the crowd. Whichever it was, times have changed. It's not just that politicians no longer seek after compromise, but that partisans no longer tolerate it.

Bob Dole's Republican credentials are beyond doubt. Along with serving in both the House of Representatives and the Senate, he chaired the Republican National Committee. He was once his party's nominee for vice president and once for president. He was active in supporting Republicans of all stripes as they sought election. Some Democrats claimed that he was overly partisan. But for all his Republican credibility, I doubt that today Bob would find it easy to win his party's nomination. I suspect that he would be opposed by the Tea Party and the Club for Growth, that they would attack him for being willing to compromise.

The large public reception room just off the floor features portraits of some of the great figures in the Senate's history. Among those luminaries is Henry Clay, known as the Great Compromiser. One wonders if anyone with such a title would be so honored today. For three decades, from the Missouri Compromise to the Compromise of 1850, Clay struggled to fashion legislative solutions that would hold the Union together before it sundered in the Civil War, nine years after his death. One of Clay's great foes, Missouri's Thomas Hart Benton, attacked him for the very idea of compromise, to which Clay responded with words that now as then uphold the legislative process:

> There are, no doubt, many men who are very wise in their own estimation, who will reject all propositions of compromise, but that is no reason why a compromise should not be attempted to be made. I go for honorable compromise whenever it can be made. Life itself is but a compromise between death and life, the struggle continuing throughout our whole existence, until the Great Destroyer finally triumphs. All legislation, all government, all society, is formed upon the principle of mutual concession, politeness, comity, courtesy; upon these, everything is based.[*]

Politics is the art of compromise. It cannot function without compromise, and it does not function today. Now let's turn to how transforming debatable politics into nonnegotiable principles, especially on questions of taxes and spending, is inconsistent with conservative principles.

Author Yuval Levin places the origin of modern con-

---

[*] Robert V. Remini, *At the Edge of the Precipice: Henry Clay and the Compromise That Saved the Union* (New York: Basic Books, 2010), 86, 87, quoting *Congressional Globe*, 31st Congress, 1st Session, Appendix, 660–61.

servatism with Edmund Burke in the late eighteenth century. As a member of Parliament, Burke had a history as a reformer who championed changes in financial and trade policy, better treatment of religious minorities, and improving the criminal law. But he thought that change should be gradual and that it should be accomplished within the structure of existing institutions so as to achieve a balance of reform and stability.* He opposed the sudden and radical transformation he observed in the French Revolution, and he believed that reform should pass through the filter of British tradition. He eschewed the notion that public policy could achieve absolute standards of perfection, and, as Levin notes, thought that politics "must consist of informed approximations."†

In other words, adherence to process was at the heart of Edmund Burke's idea of politics. Government's actions should not be a sudden force imposed on the people, but should evolve from and with respect to the nation's political and social structures. In Burke's view, the results of the evolutionary process would fall short of any concept of the ideal, but the process would avoid the tyrannical imposition of absolutes then taking place in France. Burke saw the greatest danger in people who are so certain that they possess an absolute understanding of

---

* Yuval Levin, *The Great Debate: Edmund Burke, Thomas Paine, and the Birth of Right and Left* (New York, Basic Books, 2014), 9.
† Ibid., 130.

what is best for society that they will do whatever it takes to force their vision on the rest of us.

The structure of eighteenth-century Britain that Burke believed gave stability included elements that have no relevance to the United States: the monarchy and the aristocracy. But we have our own structure, one that Britain has always lacked: a written Constitution that is the framework in which our government is conducted and our public policy is made. As the organizing principle for the father of modern conservatism was respect for societal and political structure that included the monarchy and the aristocracy, so the organizing principle for American conservatives is respect for the Constitution.

Of course, conservatives are not alone. Americans across the ideological spectrum respect, even revere the Constitution, although they might interpret various parts of it differently. But conservatives hold it especially close to their hearts, refer to it constantly, and pride themselves on being its champions. In light of the special reverence with which conservatives hold the Constitution, let's consider the question of compromise and principle.

The Constitution is both the framework of our government and the most famous example of compromise in practice. Its creation was the result of strong disagreement about how government, especially Congress, should be organized. Large states, led by Virginia, argued that their representation should be commensurate with their populations. Small states, led by New Jersey, argued for equal representation. As every child learns in civics class, the controversy was resolved by compromise. States are equally represented in the Senate, and they are represented in proportion to their populations in the House. The Constitution, so central to conservative ideology, was a practical study of political compromise. Now let's consider its content.

The body of the Constitution sets out what the federal government has the power to do. The Bill of Rights sets out what the government cannot do. The difference between the body of the Constitution and the Bill of Rights is the difference between what is on the table for political consideration and what is off the table. Article I, creating the legislative branch, includes words of empowerment: "The Congress shall have power to lay and collect taxes," and so on. The Bill of Rights begins with words of restriction, stating what Congress cannot do: "Congress shall make no law respecting an establishment of religion," and so on. Under our Constitution, some subjects are open to political decisions and others are not. Some subjects are influenced by public opinion as expressed through legislators. Others are beyond the reach of public opinion. For example, even if a huge majority were in favor of establishing a religion (which is certainly not the case), our political process would be powerless to do so. That subject is off the table for political action.

Historically, Americans have differed on how broadly to interpret the Bill of Rights. To the extent that it is interpreted expansively, the powers of the legislative branch are constrained, that is, subjects are taken off the table for political determination and defined as rights of the people that legislatures cannot abridge. The question I posed to the Supreme Court when in 1976 I argued Missouri's abortion case was this: After *Roe v. Wade,* what powers are left in the state legislature to regulate abortion? Given that the Court had held that there is a right to have abortions, was there any remaining space for legislatures to occupy, such as regulating methods of abortion and providing for parental notification?

Judicial conservatives have a broad view of legislative powers, and therefore a narrow interpretation of the Bill of Rights. Especially on questions of social values such as abortion, gay marriage, and embryonic stem cell research, they believe that decisions should result from the democratic process where legislators reflect the will of the people and not from the federal courts where judges who serve for life are insulated from popular influence. They argue that issues such as whether a fetus is a person and whether marriage is only between a man and a woman are values questions that judges are not competent to resolve, and add that when judges do decide such matters they are legislating from the bench on questions better addressed by the people's democratically elected representatives. Judicial conservatives favor a "strict construction" of the Bill of Rights—that is, before courts take matters out of the democratic process, they should point to specific constitutional language or the original intent of the framers.

Judicial conservatives are jealous guardians of the legislative process against encroachment by the courts, and in championing a convoluted, slow-moving system for deciding public policy, they are in the tradition of Edmund Burke. Congress, their favored locus of decision making, encourages and usually requires compromise in order to work. It serves the ends of conservative philosophy for Congress to function, and compromise is the means to those ends.

This is not to suggest that every compromise is laudable, and that our highest good is always splitting the differences. Of course that is not so. Compromises can be much worse than messy—they can be despicable. Consider those fashioned by the great Henry Clay in his effort to prevent the dissolution of the Union. They included extending slavery into new states and strengthening the Fugitive Slave Act. Very few people today would agree that any cause, even one as laudable as preserving the Union, would be worth the terrible price of slavery. So from our point in history we might say that congressmen of their day should have voted against the Missouri Compromise or the Compromise of 1850.

But nothing in our history is comparable to the issue of slavery. That some subjects are so profound as to be beyond compromise cannot mean that every subject is a matter of principle and closed to negotiation. Yet that has become the current state of affairs. The filibuster, once reserved for the rare case where a major cause was at stake, is now used for everything. Today, no bill comes to the floor of the Senate unless it has a filibuster-proof supermajority of sixty votes. So every budget resolution, every appropriations bill, every debt ceiling extension is treated as a threat to a fundamental principle that must be protected to the point of blocking all action. The ordinary movement of government is at a halt. The legislative process, designed by the framers of the Constitution to further compromise, is thwarted. When we take principled stands on everything, there is no forward motion on anything.

By taking an uncompromising position on that Iowa stage, eight presidential hopefuls undercut the legislative process that conservatives traditionally uphold. Instead of keeping decisions on the legislative table, they contracted the table, saying in effect that one important area of policymaking should not be open to consideration, and they did this with regard to the most unlikely subject, the imposition of taxes. Reasonable people disagree on the expansiveness of the Bill of Rights, but there is no room for disagreement on Congress's power to tax. It is the first of the enumerated powers in Article I of the Constitution. "The Congress shall have power to lay and collect taxes." To say that the power to tax is now off-limits, that it is not the subject for negotiation within the legislative process, is to remove power from where conservatives traditionally say power should reside, where it is closest to the people.

Of course there will always be, as there have always been, serious differences between liberals and conservatives over the cost of government, the weight of taxation, and the design of the Internal Revenue Code. These are differences to work out within the structure that the framers of our Constitution gave us, that is, within the Congress. To say that Congress should no longer address this question in any meaningful way, that it is not negotiable, is to depart from our constitutional system, and it is not conservative.

And, quite predictably, when a vacuum is created, a vacuum is filled. So, over the protests of conservatives, the president steps into action, increasing the power of the presidency and issuing executive orders with the explanation that if Congress will not act, the executive branch will.

Religious people who are under instruction to pay taxes even to an oppressive Caesar have a responsibility to encourage and support a functioning government. When government becomes dysfunctional, people of faith should do what they can to set it right. It may be of some use to remind uncompromising conservatives that their hardened positions make effective governing impossible and are inconsistent with the philosophy of their progenitor, Edmund Burke, but the more likely response would be the charge that we are singling out one end of the political spectrum for criticism and that we are offering nothing that is especially religious in our commentary.

With regard to the first point, I am sympathetic. I have focused on conservatives and Republicans because that is who I am. I spent twenty-six years of my life as an elected Republican. I carried my party's banner in six statewide elections. I hold traditionally conservative positions on taxes, spending, the power of government, foreign policy, and national defense, and I am an old-fashioned conservative in the Burkean sense of respecting governmental structure as the source of political change. I concentrate on conservatives because I am in the choir to which I preach. But it takes two poles to create polarization. It takes MSNBC as well as Fox News, Elizabeth Warren as well as Ted Cruz. Because politics is the art of compromise, it takes two sides to compromise, and neither side shows much willingness to do that today. So the message to liberals as well as conservatives, Democrats as well as Republicans is to avoid taking such hardened positions that politics is unworkable. To the second point, whether there is anything especially religious in this message, I think that there is. Speaking from our faith, we can help create an atmosphere where compromise is possible and government can function. Two religious principles are especially relevant to today's polarized politics: the Second Commandment and the Love Commandment.

The Second Commandment, "You shall not make for yourself an idol," seems at a glance to be irrelevant to twenty-first-century America. In its original meaning, we no longer make idols, and we don't know people who do. That is, we don't go to workshops and fashion objects out of wood or precious metals that we worship as gods. Rather than working in gold or silver, we work in opinions. We fashion ideologies and elevate them to the status of absolutes where only one God belongs. When we treat political opinions as being nonnegotiable and beyond compromise, we are entering the world of idolatry.

This is not to say that every principle of government and every rule for human conduct is uncertain and always open to debate and modification. The Ten Commandments are just that, commandments. They are stated as absolute standards of behavior. For some of them, it's possible to imagine rare circumstances where there would be exceptions—the mother who steals a loaf of bread to feed her children—but the exceptions do not disprove the rule. We shall not steal, not just most of the time or when we don't feel like stealing. We shall not steal, and that is that. Similarly, there are rules that government creates that we can take as absolutes. Child pornography is absolutely wrong, not most of the time or depending on the circumstance, but always and in every circumstance. To say that stealing violates the criminal law and that child pornography is always wrong is not to create an idol. It is not to violate the Second Commandment.

As previously noted, the effect of the Bill of Rights is to transfer certain principles from the realm of what is politically negotiable to the realm of protected constitutional rights. But even though constitutionally protected rights have been removed from political decision making, they are subject to exception. As Oliver Wendell Holmes famously said, the right to free speech does not protect one from prosecution for "falsely shouting fire in a crowded theater."*

That certain commandments and rights may be subject to exception (bread for children, shouting fire) doesn't mean that they are on a plane with ordinary opinion. They are not. Under the usual circumstances of life, they are not negotiable and open to compromise. We can state in absolute terms that people should not steal and that Americans have a right to free speech. When we el-

---

* *Schenck v. United States,* 249 U.S. 47 (1919), holding that the right to free speech does not include distributing leaflets to young men urging resistance to the draft during wartime.

evate these rules and rights into assertions of absolute truths we do not commit idolatry. Why not? What's the distinction between unshakably upholding these truths and making idols of our opinions?

The difference is that our own opinions are only our opinions, and they do not rise to the level of universally recognized values, much less divine commandments. The opinion that taxes should not exceed such-and-such a level or that spending should be increased on such-and-such a program is likely debatable. The right that one should worship as one chooses and the law against possessing child pornography are values so widely upheld as to be beyond mere opinion. Opinions are merely personal. Broadly held principles are not.

The wording of the Second Commandment makes clear the egocentric nature of idol making. "You shall not make for yourself an idol." When I make an idol, I make a god for myself. I am at the center of things. When I elevate my opinion as an absolute, I idolize my opinion and, through it, myself. I am right, you are wrong, and our differences are nonnegotiable.

Genesis teaches that you and I are made in the image of God, not the other way around. God is not made in our image, but that is exactly what we assume when we engage in the business of idol making. Humility is one of religion's great lessons. We must not place on our self-made altars our own perception of truth. And we should be especially wary when our perception of truth coincides, as it often does, with our self-interest. That is almost always the case when we opine about what government should and should not do. We think it should promote our favored programs and at no cost to us, so that becomes our nonnegotiable demand. As the great Senator Russell Long described most people's position on tax policy, "Don't tax you, don't tax me. Tax the fellow behind that tree."

The Love Commandment goes to the tone of politics as well as the content. With regard to content, it tells us that our political purpose should extend beyond serving ourselves. This is an important message from religious people, because, like the counsel of humility, religion is its principal source. Lobbyists cram the corridors of the Capitol insisting that government serve this or that private interest. People of faith have a responsibility to advocate the causes of those who do not hire lobbyists and to advance the common good.

With regard to tone, surely the commandment that we love our neighbors as ourselves includes offering political opponents enough respect to give their opinions a fair hearing. Perhaps it will prove impossible to reach an agreement on an issue, but at least we owe them a reasonable chance to express themselves. Shutting the door to compromise treats adversaries as though their ideas are worthless and not deserving of our consideration. A message from faithful people to politics is that our opponents deserve our consideration and respect. The health of American politics depends on respect for and inclusion of a variety of ideas, and it is undermined when we conclude that opposing ideas no longer matter, or, even worse, when we attack the character of people with whom we disagree.

I have a vivid memory of Sally and me having a quiet dinner in the Washington apartment of our friends Liz and Pat Moynihan. Pat was a liberal Democratic senator from New York, and a former Harvard professor who had served in the administrations of both parties. During the Nixon administration he had written a report that expressed concern about the broken state of African-American families, for which he was attacked by civil rights leaders as being insensitive and racist. I remember clearly the stricken look on Pat's face—he still felt the hurt from a quarter of a century earlier. He had tried to shed light on a serious problem, and he had been brutalized for his effort. It isn't fair to brand as racists people with good hearts who have advanced different ideas for addressing inequality. It makes dialogue impossible and progress unlikely.

I have heard and read at least a few claims that opponents of gay marriage are "homophobic." No doubt some are, but most are not nasty, just surprised. Public opinion polls have demonstrated that support or opposition to gay marriage is a function of age, with older people much more likely to resist the idea than people born after 1980. Until well along in years, people now in their seventies had never heard of it, never dreamed that marriage could be anything other than between a man and a woman. It takes some of us more time than others to get used to something new. Minds are rapidly changing on what has been a very contentious issue. It doesn't serve the cause of change to call people names.

My suggestion is that we presume the best in one another and not see dark thoughts where they do not exist. This would be in keeping with both Christian charity and good politics. Whatever the Supreme Court might decide in cases on race and gender, much will remain on the political table and much more for resolution in the human heart. The best political strategy is to bring people on board by empathizing with them, not to drive them away by attacking their character.

Politics is about inclusion, and it has been since the writing of our Constitution. Our system was designed to hold together in one nation people with very different interests and ideas. Holding together competing interests requires compromise, which is just what our complex legislative process encourages.

Religion can work either for or against compromise. Most often, especially in its dogmatic forms, it has opposed compromise. To believe that one's political positions are the same as God's and that those who disagree are God's enemies is to make negotiation impossible. Religiously fraught topics such as abortion and gay marriage are called "wedge" issues because they are intended to split us apart. A political process that values compromise allows both sides to express themselves respectfully. Because religion often insists on hardened positions, there is good reason for keeping it out of politics. Still, the meaning of religion is to bind us together and the ministry of the church is reconciliation. This means that religion's message to politics should be to respect differences, which often requires compromise.

Recently I heard a Good Friday meditation preached by the Reverend Roger Douglas, an Episcopal priest. His theme was that we all must be engaged in the world, and he said, "There are no bleachers in the Kingdom of Heaven." The reason he said this was that we are all family, responsible for one another. He concluded the meditation with a reference to the Lord's Prayer. His point should have been obvious to me, but we recite the words so often, really by rote, that their meaning can lose impact, so what he said struck me hard:

Here's a question for you. When you begin to pray the Lord's Prayer, when you start by saying, "Our

Father," who is excluded? Who do you consider not being God's child? Who is not your brother or sister?

Indeed, who is excluded? Who is not our brother or sister?

Political opponents?

CONCLUSION

What Next?

At the outset, I called the writing of this book a personal quest, an effort to work out the relationship between two subjects that have consumed me for most of my life: religion and politics. It reflects a particular point of view: I am a Republican and a Christian, and the examples I give are from my own life experiences. That said, the main points I have made are not peculiar to my religious and political affiliations. With regard to religion, I strongly believe, as Jesus taught, that there are many rooms in my Father's house. As far as politics is concerned, God isn't a Republican or Democrat, and the faithful occupy a broad political spectrum. I hope that what I have said will be helpful to people in a wide variety of faith traditions and political persuasions who share a common concern about the dysfunction of our government.

I believe that there is much we can do that can make American politics better, and that what the faithful offer is uniquely religious. In other words, if religious people remain passive, if we don't do the work of fixing politics, the work simply won't be done. We have a gift to offer America, a special gift, that we can describe under four headings:

1. Religion puts politics in its proper place, because God alone is transcendent. This is perspective that only religion can give politics, and it is perspective that is desperately needed. To grasp the need, simply tune in to talk radio or turn on twenty-four-hour TV news. What you will experience is over-the-top ranting, a blustery display of confidence that one side is absolutely right, and an Armageddon-like portrayal of the other side as absolutely wrong. Even more noticeable is the tone of desperation in the pundits who suggest that if the opposition isn't destroyed, the future of the country, maybe the world, is lost. This frantic tone is taken up by alarmed activists and opportunistic politicians who displace reasoned discussion with shouting. The message from religious people to the shouters should be quite simple: "Get a grip on yourselves. Politics isn't nearly as desperate as you say, and by making it so, you make it unworkable." I don't see that message coming from any source other than religion.
2. Religion raises our sights above the interests of self and group to concern for the common good. For our

founders, this commitment to the common good was a republican quality they called "virtue" that would be essential to the future of the nation. But virtue could not survive as a secular concept, and it died with our first four presidents. Now politics is almost exclusively in the service of self-interest—the interest of politicians in winning elections, and the interest of constituents in gaining benefits or avoiding burdens. The result is government that ducks hard decisions today and piles up huge debt for the future. While politics serves self-interest, religion pulls us toward love of neighbor. The Love Commandment is more than a part of religion, it is the heart of our witness to the world.

3. Religion is communal. As individuals become more isolated from each other, and America becomes more a collection of persons than a people, religion binds us to each other and to the whole. Of course, religion can have and historically has had the opposite effect, as we see daily in troubled parts of the world. But the ministry of religion is reconciliation, not fragmentation, and the exercise of this ministry opens creative opportunities to bridge partisan divides, change the tone of politics, encourage social interaction in Washington and beyond, and make government work. To follow through on a ministry of reconciliation would take a lot of effort, beginning with revitalizing that

great builder of social capital, our congregations. But the work of reconciliation would go a long way toward ordering the chaos of politics, and it is work that few others are doing.

4. Religion creates the environment where compromise can thrive. It warns us against turning our political ideas into idols, and it teaches us to love and therefore respect our adversaries. Successful politics is the art of compromise, but it has become a lost art as taking strident positions becomes the price of winning primary elections. The loudest voices on the public stage are the most intransigent, which means that to be effective, the voices of compromise must be at least as forceful. If the only thing officeholders hear at town hall meetings is "Don't give an inch!" then they won't dare give an inch. Citizens most supportive of compromise are least likely to have the passion to attend political meetings or even to vote, unless they believe that expressing themselves is a religious obligation. Here again, if people of faith don't do the work of promoting compromise, it's hard to see who else would do it.

These being gifts that religion can offer America, how do we equip ourselves to deliver our gifts? What do we do next? The answer must lie in both religious and political participation.

To give perspective to politics, to put it in its proper

place, we must put religion in its proper place. Because politics is grotesque when it is our ultimate concern, we must rediscover God as our ultimate concern. This means a revival of religion in America, not in the old-time sense of altar calls for Jesus, but in the sense of a renewed recognition by people of all faiths that God is transcendent, and politics is not. To create a condition where compromise is possible and government can function, we should do more than suggest that absolutism in politics is destructive—we should insist that political absolutism is contrary to what religion demands.

Religion will have little to offer politics if it is only a peripheral part of our lives. It won't have any staying power, and when we speak of it, we will have little understanding of what we are saying. If, for example, we support a politician for taking a difficult position, we should know why we are giving that support, and how doing hard things fits in with religion. Acting on our faith requires knowledge of our faith, which in turn requires both personal study and a teaching ministry.

When people say that they worship on the golf course, I doubt there's much substance in their religion except maybe the enjoyment of pleasant weather and good scenery. And something else is missing on the golf course: a congregation. As Robert Putnam and David Campbell have shown, interaction in a congregation is correlated with and probably causal to connectedness to the rest of society. If religion is to succeed in binding us together, it cannot be relegated to golf-course isolation. Religious participation should be more than individualistic. It should be congregational.

For many of us, especially those who are less aggressive, participation in politics is a taller order than participation in religion, because politics can be so hard-edged and combative. We stay away from the arguments, the meetings, and the polls. We leave the selection of candidates to the true-believing activists who care enough to make their presence felt. So the center collapses, and what is left standing is on the fringes. If we are to fix broken politics, it is essential that we not leave the practice of it to the few.

I have gone to great lengths to point out the limitations of politics, that the process is messy and the results often ambiguous, that advocating a political position is no substitute for personal responsibility. Then how can I argue for more participation given these limitations? My response is that the fundamental allegiance of Americans is to our structure of government, not to any particular ideology or policy. We take positions on taxes and spending; we join political parties; but whatever our positions and whatever our party, all of us pledge allegiance to the republic, to our system of government. No doubt the framers of the Constitution held their individual views on the issues of the day, but those issues were not the focus of their attention. Their focus was on the process of decision making, not on the content of legislation that might follow. Participants in the Boston Tea Party were protesting more than a tax on tea. They were protesting the manner in which the tax was imposed: taxation without representation. The republic to which we pledge allegiance is a complex structure for decision making that fosters compromise. While policy issues are always debatable, our constitutional structure is fixed.

The big change of the last quarter century has been that government is no longer an effective place to work out our differences, so it is not functioning as the framers of the Constitution intended. Impassioned advocates have been so insistent on pressing their agendas that they have undercut the purpose of the constitutional system. The loudest voices on talk radio and at town hall meetings don't want to work things out, and many voters in primary elections punish politicians who seek compromise. By enshrining their political positions as absolutes, they render compromise impossible, and they attack the purpose of the system that our forebears so carefully created. What America needs is many more activists in politics—not activists who work for their own causes, but men and women who are committed to the higher calling of our republic, the fundamental and profound calling of making government work.

Inspiriting such activists would be a great gift of religion to America.

Faithful people have much to offer American politics, much that can mend what is so obviously broken. But to make this offering, we will have to show up and speak up. This may seem an unpleasant prospect for many of us, but nothing in religion says that we should be content with the pleasant.

ACKNOWLEDGMENTS

A risk in acknowledgments is that they may lead the reader to assume that people who have helped along the way endorse all the author's opinions or share responsibility for errors in the text, assumptions that are certainly untrue. Readers of various versions of my manuscript have spotted errors, but could never have kept up with my capacity to make mistakes. As for opinions, I'm sure that everyone who has helped me disagrees with some, maybe many, of mine, which underscores a point I have tried to make: Political opinion is simply that, and good people can and usually do disagree with each other. Those who have helped me write this book represent a variety of religious traditions and political perspectives. What they share is concern that American politics is broken and belief that faithful people can be menders.

Two of my friends for decades have read earlier versions of the manuscript, and have greatly enriched my thinking about this book. Guido Calabresi was my professor at Yale Law School and has been my mentor for more than fifty years. The Reverend Frank Wade was my rector at St. Alban's Church, Washington, D.C., and is the wisest person I know about faith and life.

Darren Dochuk, an excellent young faculty member recently at Washington University's Center on Religion and Politics and now at the University of Notre Dame, gave me wise counsel during early stages of this project, and his wife, Debra, provided important thoughts as well. Professor John Inazu of Washington University School of Law is a scholar with a deep knowledge of law and religion who generously shared that knowledge with me.

Frank Costa Jr. was my research assistant during the summer between his junior and senior years at Yale, and he has continued to help me with research and comments since his graduation. He is remarkably gifted with intellectual depth and mental quickness. Much in this book is the product of his research.

Jon Meacham and Will Murphy at Random House have challenged me to make this book much more coherent and readable than it would have been without their input. I am grateful to them, as I am to my representative, Robert Barnett, for connecting me with Random House.

For more than twenty years since I left the Senate, Martha Fitz has been my one-person staff. Because she can do it all, and with great ability, she is the best one-person staff I can imagine.

As always, I'm thankful for my wife, Sally, for everything, including her enduring long hours of a writer's solitude.

Finally, I'm thankful for the lifelong friendship of Alex Netchvolodoff, to whom this book is dedicated. As a model of faithful living, he is an inspiration.

INDEX

totalitarians, 176
town hall meetings, 21, 148,
    199–200, 220
Trade Act of 1984, 189
Trilateral Commission, 66
Truman, Harry, 213

United Kingdom, 160
United Nations Security Council,
    137
United States:
    aid to Africa by, 72–73
    cultural identity of, 150–51
    founding principles of, 69
    Holocaust and, 61
    Panama Canal and, 21–22
    revival of religion in, 247
    Sudan peace agreement and, 73
    in 21st century, 7, 26
    world role of, 7, 72–73, 152
United States Holocaust
    Memorial Museum, 63
unity, 11, 15, 163, 240–41

values, 42, 50, 70–71, 211–12, 237
Veterans of Foreign Wars, 132
video games, 59
violence, 51, 54, 59
Virginia, 137, 228
Virginia Convention, 84–85
virtue:
    Adams on, 85–86
    Madison on, 84, 99
    Montesquieu on, 87
    Washington on, 85
    see also common good;
        responsibility
Virtue of Selfishness, The (Rand and
    Branden), 74–75
Volf, Miroslav, 139

voting:
    representative democracy and,
        18–21
    voter support and, 76–77,
        99–100, 220
    vote trading and, 89
    women's right to vote and,
        172–73

Waco, Tex., 67–68, 164
Wade, Frank, 144
Wagner, Loretto, 46–47
Wallis, Jim, 113
Wall Street Journal, 160
war, effects of, 65
    see also specific wars
Warren, Elizabeth, 234
Washington, D.C.:
    cost of living in, 184, 191
    lobbyists in, 26–27
    members of Congress in, 14,
        182, 185
    Reagan administration and,
        72–73
    support staff in, 74
Washington, George, 83, 129
Washington National Cathedral,
    143, 175
Washington Post, 23, 218
Washington Tabernacle Baptist
    Church, 167
Watergate scandal, 66
Webber, Hank, 170–71
wedge issues, 186, 241
West Point, 152
Who Are We? (Huntington), 150
Why Government Fails So Often
    (Schuck), 112
Wiesel, Elie, 60
Wilson, Darren, 161, 164

ABOUT THE AUTHOR

SENATOR JOHN C. DANFORTH, partner in the law firm of Dowd Bennett LLP in St. Louis, served in the United States Senate as a member of the Republican Party from 1976 to 1995. In 1999, Danforth was appointed special counsel to investigate the federal raid on the Branch Davidian compound in Waco, Texas. Senator Danforth was appointed U.S. ambassador to the United Nations in July 2004 by President George W. Bush. An ordained Episcopal priest, he authored the books *Resurrection: The Confirmation of Clarence Thomas* (1994) and *Faith and Politics: How the "Moral Values" Debate Divides America and How to Move Forward Together* (2006). He serves on the national advisory board of the John C. Danforth Center on Religion and Politics at Washington University in St. Louis, whose mission is to foster rigorous scholarship and inform broad academic and public communities about the intersections of religion and U.S. politics. Prior to his election to the Senate, Danforth was attorney general for the state of Missouri from 1969 to 1976. Senator Danforth graduated with honors from Princeton University and then earned a bachelor of divinity degree from Yale Divinity School and a bachelor of laws degree from Yale Law School.